Tools & Toys

Fifty Fun Ways to Love Your Class

Written & Illustrated
by
Rick Morris
Creator of New Management

For Benjamin Dean Morris,
my heaven-sent son,
who sees the world as a fun place,
and in so doing,
always wants to try new things.

For information,
you can call us at:
(619) 455-6000

or send e-mail to:
rick@teachers.net

or visit our website at:
http://www.newmanagement.com

New Management
6512 Edmonton Avenue
San Diego, CA 92122

I.S.B.N. 1-889236-01-2

Manufactured in the United States of America

Not that we are sufficient of ourselves to think of anything as being from ourselves,
but our sufficiency comes from God.
—II Corinthians 3:5

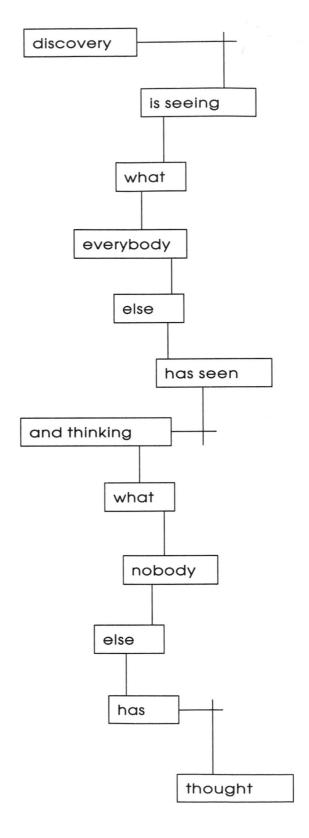

discovery is seeing what everybody else has seen and thinking what nobody else has thought

Albert Szent-Gyorgi

Acknowledgements

To the thousands of teachers I've encountered on the seminar trail during the past ten years, from all of my Mission Viejo buddies who attend the University of Will Baker to the wine country funsters of Healdsburg Union, from the hardy souls of the Copper River School District in Alaska to my hard working partners at Sequoia Elementary in San Diego, let me say thanks.

Thanks for listening to me. Even though I talk a lot and never seem to finish even when I say "One last thing," your genuine interest and support have been instrumental in keeping me focused, responsive, and on-target. Your encouragement sustains me.

Thanks for trying new ideas. It's not always easy trying new things, but it's how we get better at what we do. And, due to your willingness to take risks, I've been able to experience first hand that education is truly alive and well.

Thanks for sharing your vision of what this profession is all about. Your enthusiasm, your dedication, your love of children and teaching are a source of ongoing inspiration. I only wish the public knew the blood, sweat, and tears you put into your classrooms each and every day. You make me proud to be a teacher.

To all of the teachers, too numerous to mention by name but too special to ever forget, thanks. This book could not have been written without you.

A special word of thanks to Robert Hagan, my friend from Down Under. In the four years I've known Bob, he has shown himself to be a trusted companion, a learned adviser, and a generous benefactor. Good on ya', mate.

Table of Contents

Table of Contents

Introduction

Read me.

I know, I know. You want to get to the good stuff. But, take a moment, and read the intro. It will make the good stuff better.

Fair, Firm, Consistent

The tools and toys in this book were designed to promote and maintain two educational themes which I feel are crucial to effective education. The first one was championed at San Diego State University while I was an undergraduate working toward my elementary teaching credential. It's a simple teaching philosophy that can be summed up in three words: fair, firm, consistent. Being fair, being firm, and being consistent are probably the three best traits a teacher could possess. Unfortunately, it's extremely difficult to consistently sustain a teaching style that reflects these principles without some kind of support mechanism. It's why I use the ideas in this book on a daily basis. They are, by design, models of fairness, firmness, and consistency.

Five Basic Needs

The other important principle comes from Bill Glasser's model for motivation based upon his control theory. In a nutshell, he states that students have five basic needs which must be met in order for them to immerse themselves in the learning process. These needs are power, love, freedom, fun, and security. You will see these ideals woven into just about every tool and toy in this book. As you read, see if you can figure out which tools and toys supply which needs. Actually, since these needs are so critical to student achievement and success, you'll discover that many of these techniques incorporate more than one motivational factor. And, as you begin to use them yourself, you'll find that meeting the needs of your students will produce a high degree of involvement: the number one ingredient for effective education.

Enough philosophy; let's get down to practical matters.

Wingin' It

I've tried to keep the descriptions concise yet complete. Although I believe brevity is a blessing, I did not want to compromise the clarity of explanations by leaving out necessary details. So, if I sometimes ramble, I trust you will overlook it. Bear in mind, though, that some of the ideas might not be as fully explained as you would like. If that's the case, it's an opportunity to be creative. By allowing yourself to experiment with the ideas being presented, you'll be more likely to encounter success. So, if you find ambiguity, wing it. After all, these ideas are yours now. You own them. You—and your students—can decide how they're going to be put to best use.

Just Do It

Avoid, whenever possible, the "pretty trap." I'm referring to the feeling I sometimes get when I'd like to make something for the classroom but want it to be just right. Experience has taught me that this desire has had a tendency to postpone the actual production process. I've come to realize, though, that it's more important to get the thing made and then worry about esthetics when I have the time. An added advantage to the Just Do It Principle is that, by living with the design for a period of time, I end up with a better understanding of how to make it both pretty and practical.

Take Your Time

Be patient; education is a process. (It's not a day-by-day series of unrelated events with the goal for the day being to survive 6 and 1/2 hours with your students. We're in it for the long run.) Consequently, some of the processes and procedures we attempt to add to our learning environment might take several weeks of practice in order to be successful. But once success has been attained, these techniques will be with us for the remainder of the school year. So, as you recreate these ideas for your room and introduce them to your students, keep an open mind when visualizing time frames. Although in your head the students should have been able to figure out an idea immediately, reality and ultimate success may require 30 days and a patience touch. Tools (and more often toys) that I've wanted to throw out by the third day are working beautifully by the third week. On the other hand, if it's not working after you've given it a good run, bag it. As Justin Cunningham, Director for the California Healthy Kids program, is fond of saying: "If the horse you're riding on dies, get off. It won't do you any good to change bits or adjust the saddle."

Involve the Students

Allow the students to run or manage as many of the tools as you possibly can. Although it is sometimes easier for you do things, you can, if not careful, perpetuate a "teacher welfare" state wherein students sit back and watch. One of the objectives of this book is the development of student responsibility. Like so many other things in life, responsibility is not something that comes about with age. It must be practiced to be gained. This is why so many of the ideas are designed for the students to use. By being a necessary part of these management tools, they get to exercise and practice responsibility on a daily basis.

Student Numbers

You will occasionally come upon ideas which make use of student numbers. (Part IV, for instance, is devoted exclusively to student number tools and toys.) Each student in my room has a student number. It's used, along with their names, to identify their assignments, textbooks, and supplies. Student numbers, along with the number tools I've created to take advantage of the organizational possibilities numbers offer, are the backbone of the New Management system of classroom management and student motivation. If you're currently using student numbers, you already know how powerful this technique can be. If you're not using this type of system, merely substitute student names whenever you see numbers. The tools and toys will work just as well.

Stretching Exercises

Please don't limit yourself to what you read. Allow the ideas to stimulate your own thinking. Starburst® Math (page 37) was created by a junior high school mathematics teacher who had seen me demonstrate two separate tools: Name Tag Signs (page 57) and a ratty old lab coat I had found in a Goodwill store. I used to wear the lab coat as a motivational device for science or art or cooking or what have you. Just by donning the coat, I was transformed in something special. Well, the math teacher combined the sign idea with the lab coat and came up with Starburst® Math. Due to the power of synergy, this interactive math tool is a classic example of an idea whose whole is greater than the sum of the parts. So, keep yourself open to other possibilities. Experiment, be playful, take risks, and don't forget to invite your students to add their own ideas and suggestions.

That's enough for now. Let's have some fun.

Rick Morris
Pacific Beach, California
July 31, 1995

The Chinese ideogram for "crisis" is formed by using the characters from two others words: "danger" and "opportunity." Every crisis, big or small, presents its own danger. It's the most visible, overwhelming part of the crisis itself. The danger just seems to be staring us in the face. If, however, we are brave and sure of purpose, we will be able to defuse the danger and then act upon the opportunity which will also be present.

A simple case in point...

The candy wrappers from the Starburst® Math activity (page 37) were ending up on the floor and sidewalks outside of our room. A crisis loomed large: students were being irresponsible and showing disrespect. I had to demand action and show them that I was in charge. Instead of railing against the candy wrapper litterbugs, though, and threatening the demise of their beloved Starburst® Math, I took a different route. I announced that any student earning a Starburst® should write his name on the wrapper and deposit it in a special container. We would then have weekly drawings and award an entire pack of Starburst®—a pack contains 12 pieces—to the student whose wrapper was selected. The candy wrapper litter problem ceased that same day.

Part I
Management

Blackline Marker

With xerox machines getting more and more sophisticated, it's becoming increasingly difficult to tell the difference between my master copy and the xerox copies. This has led to a bit of unnecessary grief. If, for example, I didn't remember to separate the original from the copies I had just made in the teacher's workroom, I would sometimes end up "consuming" my original. Or, when I needed more copies of the same form, my original wouldn't be in the blackline master folder where the masters were kept. This sounds like the kind of "crisis" from which opportunity oftimes springs.

I started using a special marking pencil on my blackline masters. The pencil is called "non-photo blue" or "non-repro blue" or sometimes "Copy Not." It's the kind of pencil used by graphic artists working on camera-ready art. Marking my originals with this type of pencil has really helped.

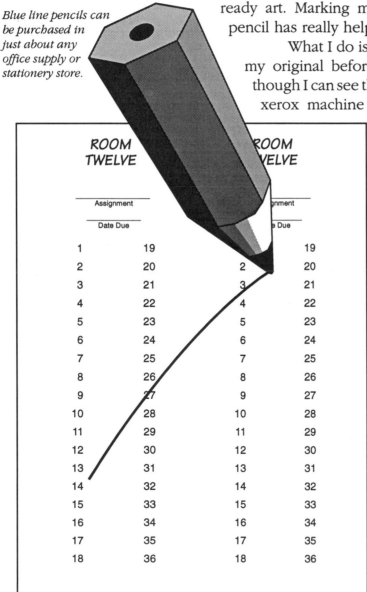

Blue line pencils can be purchased in just about any office supply or stationery store.

What I do is slash a line across the front of my original before I make copies of it. (Even though I can see the line the pencil has made, the xerox machine won't be able to. Thus, the original will show the blue line but the copies won't.) Then, when I get back to class, the blue line will remind me to replace the original in my blackline master folder. Even if I don't separate them right away—which is the case more times than I care to think—the original will still be standing out like a blue light special at K-mart.

Warning: Please test the sensitivity of your xerox machine before you slash everything you own blue. Some machines are not as sophisticated as others; therefore, they will actually reproduce the blue line.

Teacher Tip 1: If you work with partners, mark your master with your initials. This will keep the sets of papers separate and easy to return when you are making copies for each other.

Extra Papers

STUDENT:
> *Mr. Morris, I didn't get the science packet.*

MR. MORRIS:
> *We passed out those papers yesterday.*

STUDENT:
> *Yeah, I know. I was absent.*

MR. MORRIS:
> *Well, didn't your team get a set for you? Check in your paper folder or your mail box.*

(Sixty seconds later…)

STUDENT:
> *I couldn't find one.*

MR. MORRIS (SUPPRESSING THE URGE TO SCREAM):
> *MMMMMMMMMMMMMM. Just look on with one of your teammates.*

Dealing with students who never received an activity sheet has always been a pain. I've tried several ways of dealing with this issue; nonetheless, problems continued. We tried having teammates put assignments in absent folders whenever a student was not present. We also tried having assignments placed in mailboxes. Neither method seemed to work well. They required the dedicated attention of a fellow team member.

Leave it to my partner, JoAnn, to come up with a simple solution. All extra papers go into an Extra Papers tote tray. That's it. And like any process built upon the philosophy of "a place for everything and everything in its place," this assignment management technique works because we always know where extra papers can be found.

The only difficult factor involved in this procedure is making sure the extra papers get into the tote tray we've designated for this task. It's a consistency thing. Given time, it will become a habit; until then, though, you'll want to develop a routine.

Suggestions for Success:
> \> Try to place the Extra Papers tote tray within your reach.
> \> Try putting a student in charge.
> \> If papers are disseminated by team, give the remaining copies to the last team and ask them to place left overs in the Extra Papers tote tray for you.

Clipboards

A number of years ago I used some discretionary money and purchased legal-sized clipboards for the class. They came in handy for written activities when the students were away from their desks. They could work in small groups, sit outside, conduct out-of-class interviews, etc., etc. The clip kept the papers from blowing away while the smooth surface enabled them to write legibly. As one of my former students, Valencia West, so ably phrased it: "It's like a desk away from your desk." That's poetic.

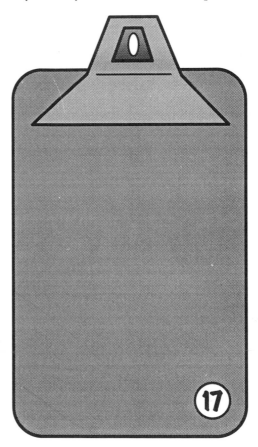

Over the years we've used them in two ways. One method was to have each student keep his clipboard at his desk. This sometimes presented a space problem for some kids as the clipboard takes up a bit of room. However, by placing it at the top of the desk in a horizontal position, it worked quite well. Not only was the clipboard available for "portable desk" services, it also served to hold and organize their activities and assignments.

This year we won't require the students to keep a clipboard. We're going to make them available for use when needed. Right now a bunch of them are hanging from cup hooks on the front edge of the chalk tray. (FIGURE 5.1) They are easy to get to and easy to replace. When you need one, take one. When you're done with it, hang it back where it belongs.

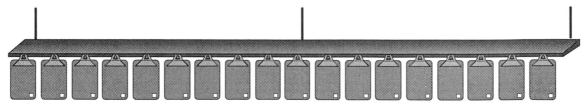

FIGURE 5.1

Bonus: The clipboards look good hanging from the tray in a long row. There are eighteen of them so they've been divided among the teams. Each team gets three. The clipboards are identified with a colored square of construction paper and a number (1, 2, or 3.) Since they occupy space which was pretty much wasted anyway, they give the impression of a well-organized, well-supplied room. And then again, maybe that's just the way I see things.

E. T. Chart

As you can see in the example below, the E.T. Chart lists activities for students to engage in when they've finished their regularly assigned material. (E.T. stands for Extra Time or Educational Time.) I've seen them in classrooms for years on end; nonetheless, when I tried my own, I experienced a bit of difficulty.

Materials:
Brass brads, a sheet of manila tag, strips of construction paper, and a large envelope.

The challenge I faced had to do with the Shortcut Principle. Kids were always looking for them. That's part of being a kid. It was my job, as the responsible, well-intentioned adult, to keep them all on the straight and narrow. Left on their own, they sometimes wandered afield. Let's use Calvin as an example.

Calvin has just finished his literature lesson. After turning in his paper and marking off this number, he returns to his seat. What now, he thinks. Oh, yeah. The E.T. chart. After studying the choices listed, he picks *Clay Sculpture*. He somehow overlooks *Learn the 8's, Write Spelling Words 5 Times Each*, and *Finish Book Report*. He jumps over all of them and lands on *Clay*. I guess I shouldn't be too surprised; working with clay is fun. Besides, if Calvin has taken care of business, I would want him to choose a fun activity. I just needed to ensure that he was completing his other assignments before having fun.

That's why I decided to reengineer the time-honored Extra Time Chart. Not for the mere sake of reinventing the wheel, but a rethinking generated by necessity.

The change I made in the E.T. chart had to do with the kind of paper I used for the activity headers. I wrote some activities on green construction paper and some of them on yellow. Any activity written on green paper meant that this was an activity you needed to do first. (If there were three green headers, as shown here, you could establish your own priority list.) When you've finished all of the activities written on green paper (or maybe worked on them for fifteen minutes or so), you would then be able to choose from the optional activities written on yellow paper. It was a simple change, using different colored paper to denote different priorities; but, since I've switched to colored headers, the E.T. Chart has worked a heck of a lot better.

Recommended: You might want to ask a student—or a committee of students—to take care of the E.T. chart for the class. Have them keep the used headers, new header paper, and the pen they need in an envelope stapled to the bottom of the chart.

Return to Sender

For as long as students have been completing assignments, there have always been those few individuals who, for whatever reasons, neglect to put their names on their papers.

3,500 B.C., somewhere in Assyria
  Teacher:
    All right. Who didn't cuneiform his name on this clay tablet?

If history is any indication of future behavior, then I think you're going to have to accept the fact that you will not be able to change this phenomenon. The best you can do is to deal with it as simply as possible.

You could, I suppose, hold the offending paper high overhead while you thunder about irresponsibility and the perils inherent from not placing proper identification on assignments. Unfortunately, though, the one student who needs to hear your dialogue is not usually listening. Bear in mind that he's the one who didn't put his name on the paper. What are the odds he's genuinely tuned into what you're saying?

Granted, with time, you'll get to the point whereby you can recognize just about everyone's handwriting. However, with all of the students who will be helping to process assignments—collecting or collating—you're going to need a simple procedure for handling the unidentifiable ones. Try this one.

Get your hands on large, see-through plastic container of some type. (Many snacks sold in bulk sizes—100-200 items—come in these kinds of containers.) Place the container in a visible, easy-to-get-to location. Announce to your students that, henceforth, all papers that do not contain some form of identification will be placed in the Return to Sender container. After that, it's merely a matter of training the students to use it. Either they're dropping a no-name paper into the container or they're checking it to see if it's holding one of their own missing assignments.

This clear plastic Return to Sender container is shown holding an assignment without a name.

Alternatives: I suppose you could designate an area on one of your bulletin boards for posting these ghost papers. Or maybe you could use the clothespins and some rope. Whatever.

Mini-Books

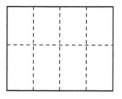

Since these fold-cut-fold books do not require any pasting or stapling, they are relatively easy for students to make. Although the first one will require a bit of patience, making subsequent books will be like forming favorite origami sculptures: they'll want to make them again and again. In fact, once they've mastered the five steps, you'll find students exploring how large and how small they can make them.

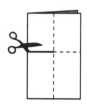

What you need:

- ☑ newsprint; 8 1/2″ X 11″
  (one sheet per student)
- ☑ scissors

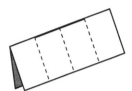

What to do:

1. Fold the paper into eighths. Unfold.
2. Refold the paper in half (hamburger fold), and cut from the folded edge to the folded intersection. Unfold.
3. Refold the cut paper in half (hotdog fold.)
4. Grasp the end panels and press the folded paper so that it forms a diamond in the middle. Continue pressing until the inside folds meet.
5. Fold the panels around and then flat so that they form a book.

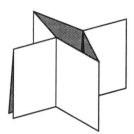

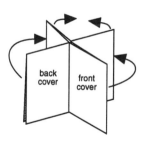

Suggested uses for your mini-books:

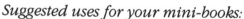

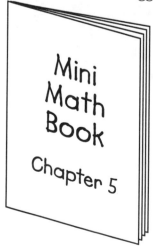

Study Booklets

I have the students make one as we begin a new chapter in the math book. As we work our way through the chapter, the students are allowed—encouraged actually—to keep notes, samples, and definitions in their mini-books. They are then permitted to use their math study booklet during the chapter final. (Since it's a timed test, they are logistically prevented from reproducing the regular math text to pore over in the hopes of passing.) These mini-math books—as we've come to call them—make for great portfolio additions.

Passports

On days when we have four or five important assignments due, we'll make mini-passports. The student will design a quick cover and then add a self-portrait on the first page. The remaining pages are used for the assignments to be collected: one page per assignment with the title written at the top of the page. Student volunteers are given a COL and a rubber stamp of some type. Everyone is then required to visit each of these volunteer collectors with the proper activity in hand. The volunteers collect the assignment, mark off the student number on the COL, and then stamp and sign the proper page in the passport. Passports are usually checked at recess and lunch time: two stamps needed for passage to recess, three for lunch, etc.

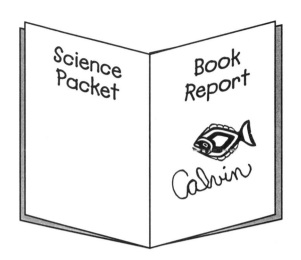

Calvin, acting as a volunteer, has collected this student's book report, stamped the passport, and signed his name. This student's science packet still needs to be given to another volunteer.

Student Book Reports

Mini-books are a perfect format for book reports. And, by assigning specific tasks for specific pages, you'll help to make the report writing process a manageable one.

Front cover: *title; author; illustration*
Inside front: *publisher; date; etc.*

Inside back: *student name*
Back cover: *your comments and final evaluation*

Page 1: *characters*
Page 2: *setting*
Page 3: *synopsis*
Page 4: *personal feelings, etc.*

Open the pages of the mini-books a bit and stand them upright on a desk or table for a very attractive Open House display.

Welcome to Open House!

Please feel free to read our book reviews.

Sarah Plain and Tall
Patricia MacLachlan

Hatchet
Gary Paulsen

Octopad

Octopad is a piece of folded newsprint that students use for math scratch paper. The reason it's folded is so that individual problems can be quickly located for visual evaluation. In the past, when my students used plain sheets for math computation, the calculations for different problems all seemed to run together in the middle of the paper like some kind of Rosetta Stone. It took forever to find the actual problem so that it could be checked. However, octopad, by design, requires students to compartmentalize their calculations. Therefore, problem 1 won't interfere with problem 2 which is free from problem 3. And thus do we achieve order from chaos.

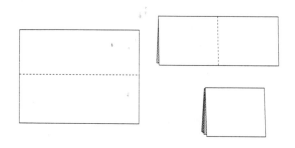

What to do:
1. Fold newsprint in half.
2. Fold newsprint in half again.

How you use:
Use the eight, separate spaces—four on the front side and four on the back—for calculations. Use a separate space for each problem you solve. Include the # of the problem in the space where you performed the calculations.

MO' MONEY MATH (A game using octopads and math activity sheets.)

Materials: math activity sheets; octopads; a digital timer; rubber stamp that produces the image of a coin; stamp pad; some type of snack.

1. Pass out activity sheets that require computation skills.
2. Pass out 8 1/2"X 11" sheets of newsprint.
3. Have students make octopads.
4. Determine how long students need to complete one problem. (Have students complete a practice problem and then stand when finished. Time them until two-thirds of the class are standing.
5. Set the timer for the desired time.
6. Give the students a problem to solve. (Don't give problems in order.)
7. Start timer.
8. As students finish, they bring you their octopads.
9. If the calculation was correct, stamp the paper and send the student back to his seats. (If the answer they had was wrong, have them circle the problem and sit down.)
10. Keep working problems until students have filled their octopads. (8 problems.)
11. Figure out a fair price for snack, and sell it to the students. (I usually start by asking how many students earned 8¢: the most you could earn if you used a penny stamp. These students usually receive several pieces of licorice. I then continue down the ranks, reducing the prize until I've taken care of everyone.)

Paper Switching Dice

If you have students exchange assignments before you correct them as a class then you might enjoy this playful idea. It's a set of dice which determines how papers are to be traded and thus eliminates the petty squabbles that sometimes occur when you ask them to switch on their own.

What you need:

- ☑ two wooden cubes (these can usually be found in old math manipulative kits)
- ☑ some type of can with a plastic lid
- ☑ permanent ink felt tip marker

What you do:
1. On one of the dice, make an **L** on three sides and an **R** on three sides.
2. On the other die, make a **1** on two sides, a **2** on two sides, and a **3** on two sides.
3. Decorate the outside of the can by wrapping a piece of construction paper around it. Ask one of the students to design some paper switching dice graphics.
4. Give the can and dice to one of your students.

How you use:

When it's time for the students to exchange papers, give your PSD manager some kind of pre-determined sign. The student will then give the can a shake, remove the lid, and read the dice inside. As you can imagine, there are six possible outcomes: one to the left, one to the right, two to the left, two to the right, three to the left, or three to the right. After hearing the announcement, your students will then know how they should switch papers.

Note: We switch papers within each pod. (See glossary.) You and your students will need to decide how the desks will be grouped so that they will know where their papers will be heading.

CORRECTION TRANSPARENCY FOR THE OVERHEAD:
   To make correcting papers more effective, I've taken to using a simple overhead transparency for posting correct answers. (You can find the master for making your own in the appendix.) Although writing 1 through 20 on board in preparation for writing the answers seems like a relatively easy matter, doing so on a regular basis can become tedious. With the correction overhead in place, you will have designated boxes for the answer you wish to write.

Tool Kits

Tool kits are heavy-duty, freezer-style ziplock bags. They are handy for holding pencils, pens, scissors, erasers, clay, clay tools, and other miscellaneous objects used by students.

What you need:

☑ Heavy-duty ziplocks
     quart size = 7″X 8″   gallon size = 10 5/8″X 11″
☑ permanent ink felt tip pen

What you do:

1. Number the bags.
2. Pass 'em out.

As you can imagine, Tool Kits are inexpensive, easy-to-use, and help to keep desks organized. They also make clean-up a breeze.

TENNIS BALL RELAYS (This play-in-the-auditorium P.E. activity is a student favorite.)

Materials: a set of 30-40 tennis balls (check Goodwill/Salvation Army); 3 or 4 five-gallon plastic buckets (check with your custodian); whistle; an incredible amount of patience

1. Divide teams into three or four groups.
2. Have them form lines for relay races. (They should know how.)
3. Give each student a tennis ball. (Good luck.)
4. Set up buckets approximately 6-8 feet away from the head of each line.
5. Give them a tossing task.

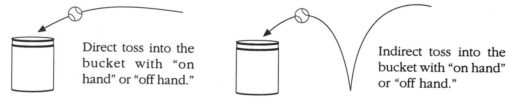

Direct toss into the bucket with "on hand" or "off hand."

Indirect toss into the bucket with "on hand" or "off hand."

(Your "on hand" is the hand you use for writing.)

6. State goal.
    > First team to have everyone complete task wins.
    > First team to have five students complete task wins.
7. Blow your whistle, and let 'em have at it.
8. If your ball goes in properly, leave it in the bucket and cheer on your team. If your ball misses the bucket, go get it, rejoin the line, and try again.

Classroom Clean-Up

Let's face it. Getting students to clean the room at the end of the day can be a bit of a hassle.

TEACHER:

> *Okay, boys and girls, let's take a minute or two and clean the room.*

Now, look around the classroom. What have you got? On any given day you'll see:

1) three or four conscientious helpers scurrying around the room setting things back in order,

2) a dozen zombie-like stiffs shuffling about in a hopeless daze trying to look as if they're doing something, and

3) most of the students doing not much of anything productive.

Although in your mind you pictured everyone happily involved in this simple cleaning process, it's just not happening. Having given this phenomenon a bit of thought, I've come to a few conclusions.

Number one, kids really don't know what to do when you say "Let's take a few minutes and clean the room." Although they will sometimes make an effort to find something to do, for the most part they are lost and confused. They need direction. They need a purpose. They need a specific task.

Another factor working against you and your mission to organize your room is the fairness factor. Many students won't make an effort to pitch in and help out unless they see that other students—especially their friends—are also doing something. Students are incredibly sensitive to issues of fairness. Granted, things won't always be completely fair; nonetheless, it's my job to make sure they are as fair as possible.

One final thought has to do with the timing of your cleaning. If you're attempting to do it just before the students are dismissed at the end of the day, their energy for leaving will probably be greater than their energy for cleaning.

Okay, now that we're somewhat more familiar with the problems inherent in the classroom clean-up procedure, how about a solution? My attempt at making clean-up workable was to create a kit for the cleaning and a procedure for using the kit. Let's look at the kit first.

The kit is composed of three parts.

1) **Task cards.** I sat down one day and came up with 32 easy-to-do tasks that needed to be completed in order for the room to returned to "normal" at the end of the day. These tasks were then written on two sheets of 8 1/2"X 11"ditto paper. (Each sheet of paper had been

folded twice both ways—see FIGURE 14.1—so that they each held sixteen tasks.) I then took these newly made blackline masters to Kinko's and had them make copies on colored card stock. (If your school xerox machine handles construction paper, use that instead.) I cut the copies so that I ended up with 32 individual task cards. The masters were saved for the display folder.

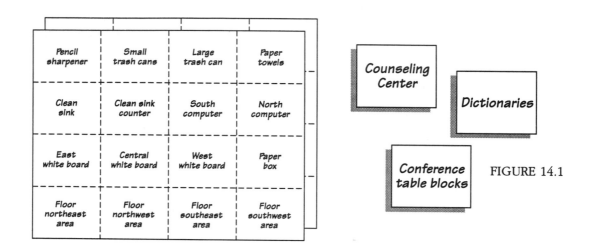

Pencil sharpener	Small trash cans	Large trash can	Paper towels
Clean sink	Clean sink counter	South computer	North computer
East white board	Central white board	West white board	Paper box
Floor northeast area	Floor northwest area	Floor southeast area	Floor southwest area

Counseling Center

Dictionaries

Conference table blocks

FIGURE 14.1

2)   **Task card container.** I found a wide-mouth, clear plastic container for holding the task cards. (They can be purchased at any supermarket or grocery store for less than two bucks.) I then made an attractive little sign, attached it to the side of the container with clear contact paper, and placed the cards inside. (FIGURE 14.2)

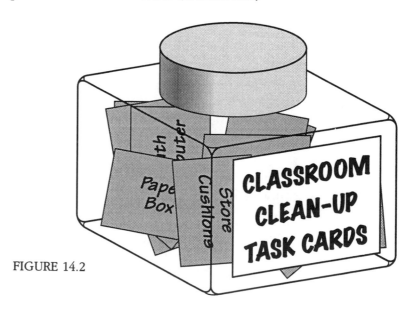

FIGURE 14.2

CLASSROOM CLEAN-UP TASK CARDS

3) **Display folder.** On the inside of a manila file folder, I glued copies of the task card sheets and then laminated it. (FIGURE 15.1)

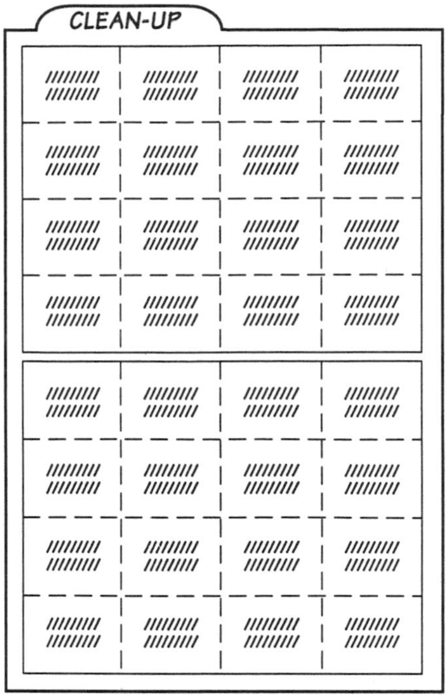

FIGURE 15.1

The Procedure. Our clean-up procedure—performed every other day—takes just a few minutes. However, we start forty-five minutes before dismissal. This allows us time for P.E. and a brief home education study session.

First, I announce clean-up by shaking the container of cards. (The sound and the visual is more effective that the verbal stuff at the top of page 13.) As students come to me to get a cleaning assignment, I pull the task cards out of the container and begin to hand them out randomly.

After receiving a task card, the student then performs the necessary cleaning/ organizing. When finished, he places the card on the proper space on the manila folder. The student then sits down and organizes his own space or asks for another task card.

After all of the tasks have been completed—three minutes max—and all of the cards have been placed on the folder, I return the cards to the container and put away the kit. We then head outside for physical education.

Note: It takes a few weeks to work out the bugs; nonetheless, it will begin to run smoothly before you know it. And once the procedure has become second nature, you won't believe how slick your room will look in just three minutes. Ours looks much better than I could make it look in twenty minutes when I used to clean-up after everyone had been dismissed.

Suggestion: As students began to learn how to complete the different cleaning assignments, I ask them to sign their names on the backs of the cards. By doing this, a student receiving a card with an unfamiliar assignment could look on the back of the card and find a student tutor.

Bold Move: Why not get a copy of the old rock-and-roll song, "Yakity Yak, Don't Talk Back," and play it during clean-up? (The first line of the song is, "Pick up the papers and the trash!") It would not only signal the beginning of cleaning but the length of the song would also establish a workable time frame for finishing.

Today Folder

My Today Folder is where I keep papers and notes that must be dealt with during the day. Announcements from the office, notes from the nurse for specific students to take home, scheduling items, etc. all go into the folder. All of the time-critical papers and forms that I find in my staff mailbox in the morning, all of the things which must be addressed when the class is actually present, all of the million and one odds and ends that I don't want to handle more than once go into the folder.

The folder normally sits in the Red Basket. (*See next page.*) If not there, it will be on the podium, the front white board tray, or one of about sixteen other possible places. That's why the folder is a special one. It really stands out. Once I locate it, I dump in everything I've just received on my pre-school trip through the office. Then, at our staff meeting (*see glossary*) I'll pull out the folder and begin to go through the papers.

MR. MORRIS (ADDRESSING HIS STUDENTS, TODAY FOLDER IN HAND):
> *Let's see here. Popsicle sale this Friday, bring your quarters.*
> *Student council meeting today at 2:10 in the student center.*

(Pause while I give the reminder to one of the council members.)
> *I see that the library will be closed this week. Brian, here's a*
> *note from the nurse for your parents. What else…oh, yeah, a*
> *thank you note from the boss (our principal) about the great*
> *job you did on the office bulletin board. Everyone was*
> *impressed with your haikus. Anything else? Nope.*

(Closing the folder…)
> *That's it. Anyone have any announcements? All righty, then.*
> *Let's get to work on those book reports, shall we?*

The folder goes back into the Red Basket. Any new items that I receive during the remainder of the day can go in the folder and be dealt with at tomorrow's meeting.

Variation: Rubbermaid makes a great clipboard/tote tray combo thing called a ClipTote. It sells for about $12 at Office Depot, comes in blue or gray, and would be perfect for using as a Today Folder.

I've got one that I used as a special "project box" during the three weeks we were working on our autumn haikus. Reminders, Check Off Lists, and sample haikus were kept on the clipboard part. Any poetry or illustrations I received during the day were popped inside so that they wouldn't be lost or misplaced. When it was time to work on haikus for the day, all I had to grab was my trusty ClipTote, and I was ready to go. It proved to be a handy, easy-to-manage tool.

Red Basket

Here's another tool enrolled in the University of A Place For Everything and Everything In Its Place. It's a red wire basket that sits on a filing cabinet right next to my desk. The sole purpose for its existence is to hold papers and things that need my attention. A short list of items might include:

> Check Off Lists and the materials being collected
> administrative circulars from the principal or office
> notes from parents to be filed or addressed in some way
> useless bits of information being routed to the teachers
> the Today Folder (*see previous page*)

By having a special place for these materials, they become easier to manage. Another advantage is the fact that it is accessible to students; therefore, they don't need to track me down or interrupt an activity in which I am otherwise engaged in order to give me some note from Mommy explaining that the family doctor said that her baby must not participate in anything physical for the next two weeks. These kinds of notes can be directly deposited into the basket where I'll see them shortly.

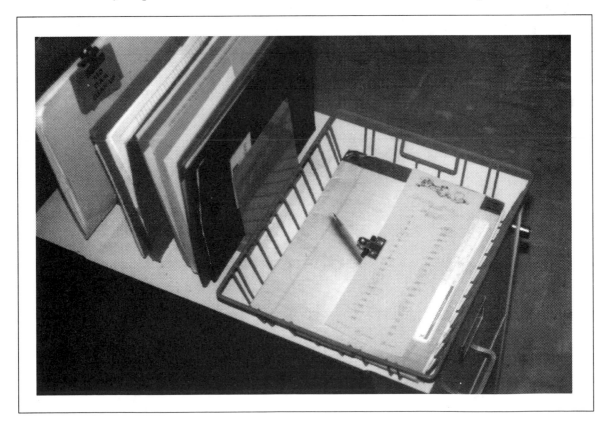

Challenge: Force yourself to have an empty basket by the end of the week. According to the latest corporate management gurus, one of the secrets of successfully dealing with paperwork is to handle a paper just one time. It's in your hand, do what needs to be done now. If left neglected, the Red Basket of Things to Do becomes the Red Basket of Things That Should Have Been Done a Month Ago.

Lining Up After Recess

I was watching my class line up on the blacktop one day at the end of recess. As I waited for the last few students to join us, I checked out our line. It was the same, rather sad, scene I had been seeing for the past twenty years.

There, at the front, were two or three children jockeying to be first in line. Behind them was a handful of kids just hanging out in line, content with their place. Then I looked at the other two-thirds of my class, the ones toward the back, talking, joking, pushing, playing, goofin'. What was so difficult about lining up, I wondered. Are they doing this just to bug me?

But then, as I continued to watch, I noticed that they weren't being belligerent or defiant. They were just being social. And that is why the line thing is so hard for students to maintain. It's tough being social when you have your back to the person behind you.

Looking off to the side, I noticed one of the circles painted on the blacktop. It was an old tether ball court and seemed to be about the proper size for what had just come to mind. I walked over to the circle, put my toes on the line, and stood facing the tether ball pole. Then I turned back toward the students and motioned for them to come join me.

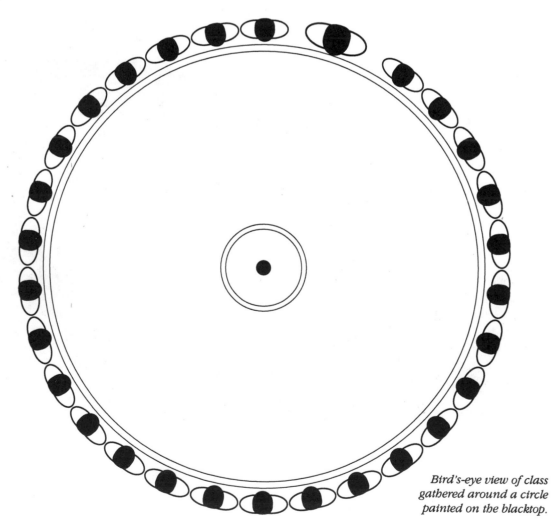

Bird's-eye view of class gathered around a circle painted on the blacktop.

The five or six paying attention walked over and stood on the circle. Within a minute or so we had everyone standing together. The circle was just large enough to hold us all so that we could stand side-by-side without having to crowd.

MR. MORRIS:

Let's line up here from now on. This seems like a better spot. Okay, follow me, and I'll lead us back to the room.

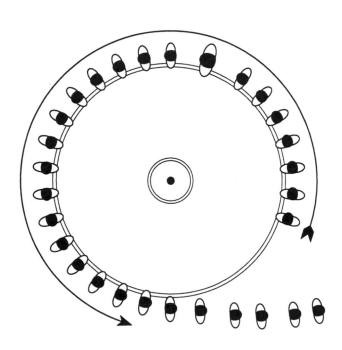

And with that, I turned to the student to my left and asked him to please wait. To the student on my right I gave the "follow me" motion. Without too much difficulty, the students peeled away from the circle and walked in single file back to class.

The next day we starting using students to do the leading. To make it fair, we decided to use student numbers and the date. For instance, on the 23rd of the month, student number 23 would be the line leader. He would also get to pick which side waits and which side follows.

Students being led back to class after recess by a student line leader.

CLAP ECHOES

In an effort to bring everyone together at the end of recess and get them focused, I will sometimes use clap echoes. By that I mean that I will clap a simple rhythm that is then echoed by the students. It's a simple idea; yet it's absolutely amazing to see students hurrying to our circle so that they can join in the fun.

Me			Them		
CLAP-CLAP	CLAP-CLAP	CLAP	*CLAP-CLAP*	*CLAP-CLAP*	*CLAP*
CLAP-CLAP	CLAP-CLAP	CLAP	*CLAP-CLAP*	*CLAP-CLAP*	*CLAP*
CLAP-CLAP-CLAP-CLAP		CLAP	*CLAP-CLAP-CLAP-CLAP*		*CLAP*
CLAP-CLAP	CLAP-CLAP	CLAP	*CLAP-CLAP*	*CLAP-CLAP*	*CLAP*

Wave Walking

As a change of pace, and a way to reinforce self-discipline, we sometimes Wave Walk to the auditorium. We call it Wave Walking because students walk in "waves," or groups. I'll first announce that we'll be Wave Walking, give them a moment to make a decision, and then start calling out the waves.

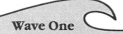

Mr. Morris:

> *The first wave is for students who wish to go by themselves. This means you will need to walk alone. You should walk quietly without disturbing any classrooms. You may go now.*
> *(Pause while they rise, slide chairs under desks, and leave.)*

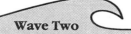

Mr. Morris:

> *The second wave is for students who wish to walk with a friend. You and your friend may walk together and talk quietly. Do not join up with other pairs of students. You may go now.*
> *(Pause for students to exit.)*

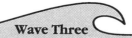

Mr. Morris:

> *This last wave is for students who wish to walk with me. We need to be polite as we walk by other rooms. Let's go.*

Each wave walks from our room to a brick planter located by the auditorium. Waves One and Two should be waiting quietly on the planter for Wave Three to arrive. We then enter the auditorium as a group.

Note: Any student who did not do well the last time he tried to walk to the auditorium with Wave One or Two would be asked to join Wave Three for this trip. With practice, though, they get it figured out.

Caveat: Since some of your students will be legally unsupervised for their journey, you may wish to discuss this technique with your administrator. (*"And exactly where were you, Mr. Morris, when Calvin walked into the pole and sustained a concussion? Well, your honor…"*) I just know how important it is for students to be given a chance to show they can be self-disciplined on their own. How about posting a student "life guard" to help out?

Minute of Silence

The average school day consists of approximately 400 minutes. This idea has to do with the last one. I'm referring to that final sixty seconds before everyone bails out of the room and heads home.

How about making it a minute of silence? It could be used as a time to reflect upon the day or merely establish a serene atmosphere for dismissal. Whatever your ultimate purpose will be—and you'll find it changing as you try this simple yet soothing technique—spending the last minute of the day in silence will have a wonderfully calming effect upon your students.

> MR. MORRIS:
> *Everyone rise please, and slide your chair under your desk.*
> (Pause for compliance.)
> *Sixty seconds of silence beginning ......now.*
> (Wait for one full minute.)
> *School's over; go home.*

To begin with, you might want to try just fifteen seconds of silence. That doesn't seem like a terribly long period of time until you actually do it. Stop reading and give it a try. Sit quietly for fifteen seconds. As you do this, picture yourself in front of your students as they wait silently. It was longer than you imagined, wasn't it?

After a week or so of fifteen seconds of silence, move up to thirty. Within a month you'll have them patiently holding still for the full minute.

Caution: Avoid the very real temptation of invading the silence with some last second announcement or reminder. The success of most classroom ideas is predicated upon your own participation and respect for the rules.

Intervention: For those students who are going to challenge you by being less than silent, try standing next to them before asking them to stand silently. If that doesn't work, speak with them after class.

Gettin' Tough: Another way to deal with a recalcitrant group would be to stop timing, repeat your request for sixty seconds of silence, and start timing a new minute. (Try using a digital stop watch.) Given time, even the most jaded of souls will refrain from interrupting the peace with their noisome presence.

Part II
Motivation

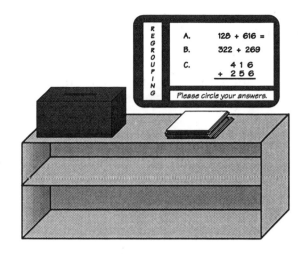

The Bonus Box

The Bonus Box is a simple classroom activity for encouraging your students to face the challenge of mathematics during their spare time. The puzzles presented—which sounds better than problems presented—are such that they can be completed in less than fifteen minutes. By allowing your students the opportunity to focus on just a single aspect of math for a brief period of time, you will encourage them to master critical math skills in a manageable way.

The first step is to set-up a Bonus Box area. The top of a book case placed near a wall will do. Set your Bonus Box[†] and some scratch paper on the top shelf. Mount a small bulletin board on the wall for pinning up your Bonus Box puzzles.

Create your puzzle on a piece of 12″ by 18″manila drawing paper. Sometime during the beginning of your day, introduce the puzzle to your class. Encourage them to understand what the puzzle represents in a mathematical sort of way. Provide a bit of time for them to verbalize important concepts: how to visualize the puzzle, how to show computations, labeling answers if necessary, the inclusion of dollar signs and decimal points, etc., etc.

Allow your students time to solve the puzzle during the course of the day when they have free time in which to think and work. We call this E.T., or Educational Time. (*See E.T. Chart on page 6.*) Since some of your students may wish to work together on these puzzles, you might want to discuss and decide that issue together.

The next day, at the beginning of your math lesson, take down yesterday's puzzle, and clip it to the chalkboard. Solve the puzzle as a class activity: a great way to review the previous day's math lesson. Also, you'll be using the entire class to help process an extra credit assignment which, in a way, it is. Write the answer(s) on the board for reference.

Have someone bring you the entries from the Bonus Box. (Have them also stick around to unfold them due to the high incidence of "origamied" puzzle entries.) Check each entry and announce names of correct solvers. After all entries have been checked, pass out coupons to the winners.

[†] *Tips on putting together your own Bonus Box:*

• Keep it relatively small and very sturdy. Find a box or something with a lid or top that opens easily. Decorate it somehow. Make it special.

• Cut a slot in the top for slipping in entries. I've found that my students thoroughly enjoy stuffing their papers through that opening. It's a Calvin & Hobbes kind of a thing.

18	////
19	
20	//
21	////
22	///
23	
24	////
25	//

Opportunity: Using a Check Off List, have one of your students keep a stick tally record of the correct solvers. By doing this, you'll end up with a simple record of who is solving these mathematical challenges: a partial indication of their effort in math.

Wall of Fame

The Wall of Fame is a special bulletin board that we use as a sort of scrap book for the year. On the first day of school it's blank: all twelve feet of it. (Actually, it's covered in butcher paper and has a Wall of Fame title at the top. Other than that, though, there's nothing on it.) Then, as the year progresses, we start to add items.

> pictures
> awards
> thank you notes
> mementos
> art work
> special event buttons
> ribbons

> Good Citizen photos
> field trip photos
> around school photos
> and a ton of other stuff

After cutting out letters on the Ellison Die Cutter, "float" them above the board with straight pins.

"I Made a Good Choice" cards are stapled on the Wall after they've been signed by the folks. The 10 objectives come from the portion of our report card that deals with work skills and study habits. (Blackline master in appendix.)

I MADE A *GOOD CHOICE*

Name: _____

Date: ___/___/___

BEGINS WORK PROMPTLY
COMPLETES WORK ON TIME
WORKS COOPERATIVELY
FOLLOWS DIRECTIONS
DOES NEAT, CAREFUL WORK
CLASSROOM BEHAVIOR
PLAYGROUND BEHAVIOR
RESPECTS RIGHTS OF OTHERS
PRACTICES SELF-DISCIPLINE

I made a really good choice today in class. Making good choices is making me a good student and a better person.

At the conclusion of our Good Citizens' assembly, the award winners have their pictures taken and posted in the office. We also receive a copy of the photos which are added to the Wall of Fame.

One of the most important parts of the Wall of Fame is that it reflects the students. It's not some labor-intensive, content-heavy, curriculum-inspired designer showcase.

It's us: Room Twelve, Class of 1992 or '95 or whatever year it happens to be. It wasn't up there when we walked in the first day of school, and it's going to take all year to create; but, boy isn't it something? That's us up there on that wall. I like that. I like it a lot.

Photographs are some of the best additions to our Wall of Fame. To make them more interesting, I've taken to cropping them on the paper cutter. The result has been a mosaic of intense photo moments.

You might want to allow your students to bring cameras (and film!) to school to shoot various parts of your day. You end up with some candid shots without having to pay for film or processing. An added bonus is that your photo journalists gain from having their work published on the Wall.

P.T.A. buttons for special events are pinned up in one corner of the Wall. We usually keep the annual ones such as this school olympics pin from 1991.

Patches look pretty slick hanging on the Wall of Fame. This one was given out for the California Physical Fitness Program. Check with your students to see if they've received any for their sports, hobbies, or personal pursuits..

If your class doesn't win any ribbons, check with your students to see if they've won any. Other than that, you can make your own ribbons for whatever reason you wish.

Student of the Day

Blackline master in appendix

We usually pass out the Student of the Day award at the end of the day. As the students sit silently for sixty seconds, I grab a certificate and a pen. The sixty seconds of silence give me enough time to think back through the day and come up with some appropriate bit of behavior or achievement to recognize. With a fat felt pen, I print the student's name and then add my signature. When Max beeps at the end of the sixty seconds, I'm ready to give the award.

First, the student who received the award yesterday brings me the trophy. (This trophy has been sitting on the winner's desk all day.) Then I begin verbalizing the behavior or achievement for which the award is being presented today. After a brief spiel, I identify the student. He or she then comes up to receive the trophy and certificate. The class can usually be counted on to applaud politely. All in all, it makes for a nice finish to our day.

Even though this is just an old bowling trophy donated by a parent, the label on the front says it all: Student of the Day.

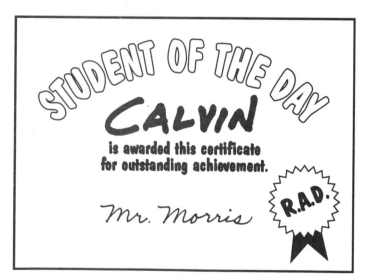

The initials R. A. D. stand for "Responsible and Dependable."

Note: The Student of the Day certificate *(above)* has been a recent addition to the award process. For years we had given out just a trophy. Many of the students, though, had been asking if they could take the trophy home at the end of the day. Obviously, they wished to share their success with their families. Since I didn't want the trophy leaving the room, we decided to present a certificate along with the regular trophy. Now, with paper in hand, they're free to let Mom and Dad know what a great kid they were that day.

By the Way: The certificate does not need to be returned; although, if it is, I don't see why it couldn't be added to the Wall of Fame. Or, maybe you could dedicate some special, unused space just for them.

Photo Tags

Photo tags are xeroxed copies of student photographs that we pin near assignments and activities that are being displayed on bulletin boards. There is something both personal and powerful about actually seeing the student's face appear next to his work. Granted, you can see the student's name on the assignment when you get close to it; nonetheless, the face is more immediate, more engaging, and more playful.

What to do:

1. Take portrait-style photos of your students.
2. On the paper cutter, trim each photograph so that it measures 3 1/2"X 2 3/4".
3. Create sheets of photos by laying them out in three rows of three and then taping them together on the back side.
4. Make 5-6 xerox copies of each photo sheet.
5. Cut the copies and place individual sets of photo tags in envelopes.
6. Distribute sets to students.

Photo tag of student shown actual size.

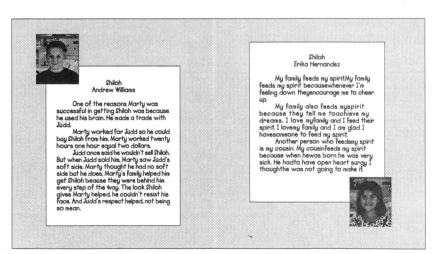

Bulletin board displaying student assignments and the photo tags of the authors.

Coupons

Everybody likes the chance to win something. It doesn't really matter what the prize is. It's the suspense and drama and mystery of it all that creates and maintains interest. Over the years, I've found that raffle coupons are a great way to offer your students the opportunity to win something.

As a student receives a coupon, he tears it in half. One half is deposited into a raffle container and the other half is kept. (Since you need to have the matching half in order to claim your prize, the handling of coupon halves becomes another exercise in responsibility.)

Coupons are drawn at appropriate times during the day throughout the week. I usually end up drawing anywhere from eight to ten coupons in all.

After reading the number, the student with the matching number stands and reads the number back to us. After confirming a match, the student writes his name on the coupon and pins it on our Wall of Fame *(see page 26)*.

The prize, given out on Friday, is most often something to drink. I'll go to Vons and find six-packs of soda on sale. I'll buy one or two, depending upon how many coupons I want to draw, and then have them icy cold by Friday morning recess. After recess, when everyone comes in to do silent reading, the winners are given their drinks.

After the prizes have been given out on Friday, all coupons in the container are dumped! This requires that students continue to exhibit appropriate behavior and achievement. No one gets to kick back because they already have a fistful of coupons in the raffle jar.

There are a couple of reasons why coupons are particularly rewarding. The first is the fundamental way in which the students are recognized for their behavior and achievement. Due to their nature, a coupon is no guarantee of a prize, just the chance to win a prize. Thus, I can follow the dictates of Maslow who espouses the intermittent reward as the most effective form of behavior modification. I can pass out all of the coupons I want for whatever reasons I wish. Whether you actually win something is up to fate. When the hand of providence reaches into the jar to select a winning coupon, you might win, but then again you might not.

Another bonus to using the kind of coupons I recommend—the ones with numbers on both ends—is the suspense factor. When a coupon half is pulled, the six digit number is read to the class. Slowly. One digit at a time. They'll be with you all the way, checking their

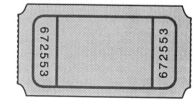

numbers for a match. When I used to use slips of paper with student names on them, a lot of the drama was lost.

> MR. MORRIS (DRAWING A CAUGHT BEING GOOD PAPER AND READING A NAME):
> *Brian!*

Well, Brian's thrilled but the rest of the students didn't get much out of it. The whole thing was over before most of them even realized I had drawn a winning slip of paper. However, if I'm reading a number…

> MR. MORRIS (READING THE NUMBERS FROM A COUPON STUB PULLED FROM THE CONTAINER):
> *6…7…2……5………5………3!*

It's a whole different ball game.

Note: Giving out drinks on Friday is just one way to reward your students. It is certainly not the only way. In fact, there are a wealth of reward opportunities available in your room or on your campus that won't cost you a cent. Talk it over with your class and see what they would like to see offered as prizes. They might just surprise you with what they come up with for rewards.

Important factor: If the prize might be different from drawing to drawing, you need to be prepared for someone not being entirely enraptured with what they've just won. That's one reason the drinks work well: everyone is receiving the same thing. That's fair. Also, it's something to ingest and students, for the most part, are always hungry. If, however, one student receives a drink but the next receives ten minutes of free time, someone might feel as if they had been ripped off. My suggestion would be to allow the students to choose their prize from a list of prizes. That way, everyone gets what he wants, which is the ultimate prize.

Extension: As opposed to reading the numeral on the coupon as six separate digits, you could read it as an actual number. So, instead of 6-7-2-5-5-3, you could say, "Six hundred seventy-two thousand, five hundred fifty-three." I tried this with my third graders when they were learning how to read large numbers. It was amazing how quickly they got it down when an icy cold drink was on the line. Read the number correctly, the drink will be yours on Friday. Read it incorrectly and your coupon goes back in the container. Tough, but fair.

Team Coupons: As sometimes happens when you use coupons as part of your system for rewarding behavior and achievement, you find yourself having to deal with the students who are verbalizing their displeasure at not holding the winning coupon.

To help students develop the ability to celebrate someone else's success, I occasionally announce that the next coupon drawn will be a team coupon. That means that whoever holds the winning half will be earning a prize for everyone on his team. This simple variation makes it a bit easier to genuinely applaud the fact that someone else has had their lucky number called out. With practice and a bit of time, though, your students will embrace the concept that they just aren't going to win each and every time.

Student Bulletins

Blackline master in appendix

There's nothing terribly new about this communication tool; I just like the way this one looks. It has a very friendly type face which the parents seem to see as warm, sincere, and non-threatening. Even the worst news, when wrapped in an attractive package, will be bearable.

STUDENT BULLETIN

Name _____   Date _____

BEHAVIOR

❑ Demonstrated leadership
❑ Set good example
❑ Strived to improve
❑ Sometimes forgot self-control
❑ Placed on restriction
    for one day

❑ If checked here,
    please sign & return.

WORK SKILLS

❑ Worked independently
❑ Showing improvement in
    work skills and study habits
❑ Needed some guidance to
    complete class assignments
❑ Needed constant guidance to
    complete class assignments
❑ Easily distracted
❑ Distracted others

EFFORT

❑ Excellent effort
❑ Very good effort
❑ Good effort
❑ Is improving
❑ Needs to improve

Conference requested
❑ by teacher
❑ by parent

Teacher signature _____   Parent signature _____

These bulletins are somewhat easier to handle if you have them gummed up into pads of 50 sheets or so. Kinko's, the copy place, will not only make the copies but will cut and pad them for you.

Here's a slight variation that might make using these bulletins more manageable for you. Instead of filling out the entire bulletin yourself—name, date, note on back—try having the students do it for you. As you give a student a bulletin, verbalize the reason it is being issued. Ask him to write a note to his parents about his accomplishment on the back of the bulletin. Ask also that name and date be filled in. Leave with the understanding that the student will see you later in the day so that you can check appropriate items and sign your name. By doing this, you will save yourself time and energy so that you can "bulletin" other students. More importantly, though, you'll be involving students in the validation process. It's actually more significant, in the long run, for them to develop their own feelings of success than for me to do so.

General rule: I don't try to evaluate each student on a regular basis; i.e., a student bulletin does not go home for everyone at the end of the day or week. I've found that I am not completely accurate in my evaluations if I am forced to do so because of a time line. Evaluations will eventually loose their meaning and thence their value if they are not genuine.

The Neon Necklace

The Neon Necklace is a quick and easy way to visually check your students to see who has turned in a special assignment and who stills needs that extra bit of intervention.

I made a set of necklaces from neon-colored shoe laces. I took each one and tied its ends together. I ended up making about forty of them. After making the necklaces, I hung them from the back of my director's chair.

Using them is easy. First I'll announce that we'll be collecting some important assignment that day. For instance...

MR. MORRIS (MAKING AN EARLY MORNING ANNOUNCEMENT):
Book reports are due today by 2:00. Please place your report in the folder, and mark off your number on the Check Off List. After you've done that, come see me. I've got a Neon Necklace for you.

As students turn in their book reports, they come to me for a Neon Necklace. After receiving their necklaces, they put them on. Some kids wear them around their neck, as designed, while others will wear them around their wrists. Either is fine as the necklace is visible.

Everyone benefits from the Neon Necklace. For my students, it becomes a badge of honor. The necklace shows that the wearer has taken care of some special task. And, since kids want to be like their friends, they work hard to be able to wear one.

The benefit for me is obvious: I no longer have to guess which students aren't finished yet. I just look for a necklace. Anyone without a necklace still needs a bit of encouragement about completing and handing in their reports.

At the end of the day all necklaces are collected and hung on the director's chair until we need them again.

Caution: In order to maintain the novelty and effectiveness of this tool, I don't use it very often. Once every couple of weeks and only for an important assignment.

Teacher Tip: To prevent young children from chewing on them, offer them a simple reward at the end of the day for turning in a dry necklace.

Reward Tube

For years on end I've thrown away Check Off Lists when they had served their purpose. Everything collected, everyone marked off? Great. A quick crumble, a quick toss, and that was that.

Then I gave up the idea of throwing them into the trash can and began to exercise the Use It More Than Once philosophy. The wadded up COL's were now going to end up in the recycling box so that the paper could be reused by someone. Progress.

But now, instead of merely tossing them away, we've taken to saving them in a clear plastic tube as a form of motivation and reward. After all, that completed Check Off List represents a lot of effort on the part of our class—the students *and* me—and it seems kind of a shame to just toss it away like so much junk mail. Is there an opportunity lurking about? I think there is.

What you need:

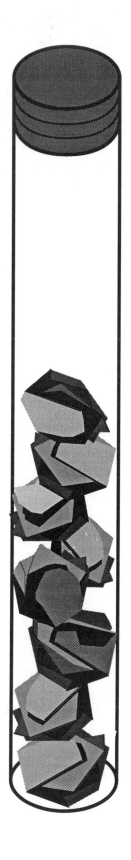

☑ One clear plastic tube approximately 2″ in diameter and 15-18″ in length.
(Ours was the container for a wall calendar. You might want to try using the clear plastic cans that hold tennis balls. You can usually find these strewn about at any public tennis court.)

What you do:

Announce to your class that you are going to begin saving Check Off Lists that have been completely marked off. Then show them the tube you will be using for saving your COL's. After that, decide what kind of reward your class will receive when the tube is full. (It's up to you how you do this. You can do it yourself or involve your students.) After you have reached or announced your decision, drop the first wadded-up Check Off List into the tube. (Experience has shown that you really need to crumble up the lists or have something on hand to ram them to the bottom of the tube. Maybe you should practice once or twice to see how your paper reacts to your tube.) After depositing your first completed Check Off List in your tube, put it on display somewhere in your room.

The only thing left to do is continue adding finished COL's to the reward tube until you've reached the top. (It's great to see them pull together to take care of some Check Off List item as the stack of crumbled ones nears the finish line.) After you've provided your predetermined reward, make a ceremony out of emptying the tube and starting over.

Possible rewards for filling the tube:

> *Fifteen minutes of extra recess*

To help make this a manageable and more effective reward, I have begun to allow them to decide when, during the day, they would like the extra time. In the past, it was normal to tack on the extra fifteen minutes to the end of the regular morning recess. Now I'm thinking that a completely separate time would make for both a better break and an increased awareness of the fact that the time came from filling the tube.

> *Fifteen minutes of in-class E.T., or Extra Time*

> *Their choice for a physical education activity*

> *A class cooking experience*

> *A no-home education night*

I'm not completely convinced that we should make getting out of a home learning experience one of our rewards. It's rather counterproductive in the long run; nonetheless, I know I wouldn't mind receiving a *Get Out of One Staff Meeting Free* card from my principal in recognition for some helpful deed I had managed to pull off.

> *Whatever is appropriate for you and your students*

ALTERNATE STUDY AREAS:

We have a number of places in the room where students can go to complete their activities. In addition to the Counseling Center (a double desk) we keep a desk outside the door. We also have two large tables at the back of the room we use for conferences, small group meetings, or team stuff. Any of these places, when not occupied, can be used by a student. They don't even need to ask; they just go. The idea is to offer them the freedom to choose a more productive environment in which to take care of business. Otherwise, they're sometimes left to verbally duke it out with a troublesome neighbor.

Rainbow Handwriting Award

Students like awards and recognition. It's why I try to have several that are given out on a regular basis. For instance, every Monday we identify two Students of the Week. Their names appear at the top of our Home Education Bulletin and a special pennant trophy sits on their desks the entire week. Additionally, at the end of each day, a Student of the Day is selected. *(See page 28.)*

A mug o' markers is all you need.

The Rainbow Handwriting Award, another of these regularly awarded honors, goes to the student who is either using great handwriting or is truly improving in handwriting skills. As I look through assignments, I'll add names to a list of students who should be recognized for their efforts. Just before we begin Daily Oral Language, I'll check the list, read a name, and present the award.

The actual award is a coffee mug—one of the 400 I've received over the years as presents from students—filled with Crayola brand felt markers. The student receiving the award is allowed to use the markers for the day. At the end of the day the award is given back (Since I don't always remember to give it out, it's important that the mug and pens are returned promptly. It might lose some of its significance and desirability if the award has been sitting on someone's desk for a week, if you know what I mean.)

Something new: Another way to make the Rainbow Handwriting Award special would be to fill the mug with the new Crayola Mini-Stampers. This set of eight washable markers ($3.98) has special tips that work like rubber stamps. The eight shapes—star, heart, foot print, paw print, swirl, star burst, lips and happy face—make for a unique felt pen experience.

Suggestion: Keep the pens cap down in the mug. They won't dry out as quickly as they normally do.

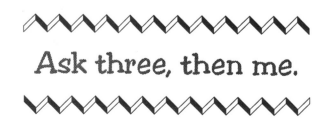

Classroom sign which encourages students to first check with fellow students for answers to simple questions before asking the teacher.

Starburst® Math

Starburst® Math is an interactive math activity that's fun for me and the kids. And, like the Bonus Box idea, this one stresses accuracy and mastery of math skills in a manageable way.

What you need:

- ☑ lab coat
  ($3-5 at Goodwill stores)
- ☑ plastic name tag holder
- ☑ construction paper
- ☑ felt tip pen
- ☑ Starburst® candy

Starburst candies go here.

Student answers go here.

What to do:

1. Cut construction paper so that it fits in name tag holder.
2. On one piece of paper, write a math problem.
3. Insert the paper in the name tag holder, and clip it to the lab coat.
4. Fill the right pocket of the lab coat with Starburst® candy.
5. Wear the lab coat.

How you use:

Announce to the class your newest math idea. Show them the problem in the name tag—you might want to write it on the chalkboard for your demo—and the Starburst® candy in your right pocket. Let them know that a Starburst® is theirs if they can correctly solve the problem. All they need to do is write their solutions on a piece of scratch paper and place in the left pocket of the lab coat. Remind them about including identification on their paper.

As you walk around the room doing whatever you normally do, students will come up to you with their answers. Hold the pocket out so that they can insert their papers. Pull out a paper every now and then, and check the answer. If done properly, pay a visit to the student and offer him a choice of Starburst® candy. (In our room you get one, but you do get to choose the flavor.) Toss the answer sheet, and carry on with your activities.

When you pull out an answer that was not done correctly, see the student and offer a quick mini-lesson. Suggest they try again. They'll be back before you know it.

Opportunity: In order to give your students practice at problem solving while eliminating the need for you to write some complex math tale on a piece of name tag paper, just write down the number of a problem from your math book and the page on which it is found. For example, **#8 on page 120**.

Music

Forgive me for being such an opinionated guy; but, you gotta have music in your room. Whenever I play music—and many times it's when I'm alone taking care of business—the room is a much more pleasant place in which to be. I find myself spending more time grading papers, preparing lessons, etc. when the place is jumping. Music makes a lonely classroom come alive.

The students also find music to be a great addition to the room environment. After all, music is a big part of their lives. They're very comfortable with tunes. In fact, I think they are actually more calm when we have a tape playing. (This is especially true if your students are allowed to be in the room before school begins.) And it doesn't really matter what type of music is on. They appear to be less anxious, less self-conscious, and not so inclined to make their own noise to break the tension that sometimes occurs in a silent room. It's almost as if the music masks their presence. They're free to move about and talk without feeling as if everyone is focused on their activities.

Try this experiment when you are alone in your room. Play a bit of music. Play something you like. Wander around the room and do a few things. Now turn the music off. Seems kinds of empty, doesn't it? Feels like something is missing, don't you think? Music: you gotta' have it.

Suggestions for Success:

> Use a decent cassette player, a boom box if you will. The sound quality is worth the investment. Also, by playing tapes instead of the radio, you'll avoid bad disc jockeys and irritating commercials. You can more easily control a tape deck or CD player.

> Try turning on the music as soon as you enter the room. It's just amazing what a boost to the room environment music makes. If your students come into the room before school begins, have the music on for them.

> Put a student in charge of turning off the tape player when the bell rings to start your day. I've found that the absence of music is more of a cue than the bell itself.

> Play a variety of music. Classical, jazz, rock-and-roll, even opera, make for fun listening. Offer to play tapes the students bring in. This will promote ownership and involvement. I recommend that you ask students to screen the lyrics of their music for profanity, violence, or sexually explicit content. Although they're pretty good about bringing in appropriate music, I always ask: "Any sex, swearing, or violent thoughts on this tape? No? Let's pop it in and play it."

> Play music at a variety of times during the day. I'm always willing to trade their talking during a work session for some music. Contrary to popular belief, students actually become quieter when music is played during independent activity times.

Clay in a Can

Here's a simple E.T. activity that is a wonderful right brain stimulator. It's nothing more than modeling clay. What keeps it simple is the manner in which the students store their clay. The clay is kept in an empty 35 mm film canister. This not only makes it easy to keep inside of a student desk or Tool Kit but also limits the amount of clay you have. (I have found that students don't need much at all to create their sculptures.)

Working with clay during our after lunch story time has become a time of real artistic development. The time frame—15 minutes— is just enough to allow them time to fashion something detailed. Many times I give them a sculpture assignment from the story I'm reading. (You should have seen the teepees and campfires they created when I was reading *The Indian in the Cupboard*.) After I've finished reading, we'll take a moment and walk around the room to see what other students have sculpted. The clay is then cylinderized and canistered.

In the beginning, they had a rather difficult time squashing their creations and rolling the clay into a cylinder for reinsertion into the canister. This was especially true when they had made something that they really liked. I had to convince them that their little pony, or rocking chair, or alien head, or whatever they had just created would still be a part of their clay; they just had to bring it back out again.

Warning: Unless the clay is neatly reformed into a cylinder, your students will have difficulty extracting it the next day. If it's just jammed in, the clay will want to stick to the sides of the film canister. The only recourse is to scrape out your clay with a tool. Once the sides of the canister have been coated with a layer of clay, it will never come out cleanly. You might want to have extra canisters on hand. And, since you can get these by the gazillion at just about any film processing place, having extras is doable.

CLAY TOOLS

As your students become more confident sculptors, they're going to want to have some tools for detailing and texturing their work. Popsicle sticks shaped on the sidewalk, straightened paper clips, nails from home, plastic utensils, etc. make for handy tools and can be easily kept in their Tool Kits.

Part III
Interaction

Signed English

According to the research, 80% of the talking done in the elementary classroom is done by the teacher. That's a lot of talking. In fact, if we're not careful, the voice that does all of that talking will actually become invisible to the students after a time. The way I see it, anything we can use to replace our voices—sound makers or Signed English—is worth whatever student training effort is required to make it a part of the classroom language.

Signed English, for me, started about seven years ago. I was teaching a math lesson to my third graders. We were three days into a combined perimeter/area session. Having covered the concept of perimeter for the past two days, I wanted to do a quick review as a natural seque into the day's lesson on area. I drew a rectangle on the chalkboard and labeled the sides. Turning to my students, I posed what I thought was an appropriate question.

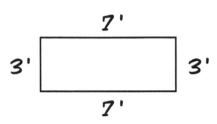

MR. MORRIS:

What is the perimeter of this shape?

(Six hands were quickly raised. One of the hands, as it turned out, belonged to one of my underachievers. [We'll call her Stephanie for the purposes of demonstration.] Being an underachiever in math and having her hand raised for what I thought was an answer to my question, I wanted to allow her a chance to showcase her newly developed math skills. I wasn't prepared for her response, though.)

Stephanie?

STEPHANIE:

What's perimeter?

Yikes. Where did that question come from? Here I was, all ready to have Stephanie reinforce the fact that I can teach math to even the most underskilled of students, and she blindsides me with a question that shows she has no real understanding of what we've been talking about for the past two days.

Instead of answering her question, I put her on hold and went to one of the other eager hand-wavers for the answer. Not very fair to Stephanie, but my expectations of hearing the right answer hadn't been met. Also, I was kind of hoping that Stephanie might get something out of the student who did offer the correct response. Probably the only thing she got out of the entire interchange was: "Don't ask questions. They get in the way of the lessons." Ouch.

Later in the day, as I reflected on the situation I had faced during math, I came to the realization that my treatment of Stephanie's question had more to do with the fact that I hadn't been expecting a question. It wasn't a lack of desire to help my students become the well-skilled young people that I want them to be. It was the surprise that threw me, and I don't always deal well with classroom surprises. If I had somehow known that Stephanie had a question before I called upon her to respond, I would have been more than happy to do some reteaching.

I went back to class the next with an idea in mind. A friend of mine had been teaching his students the Signed English alphabet. Students who had mastered this skill were given time each day to engage in what they called "Z Talk," or conversation through signing. No talking, just signing the letters that formed the words you wanted to share with your friend. If Signed English worked for his class, maybe it would work in mine.

I demonstrated to my students how to form the letter "i" and asked them to please use this sign in the future when they were raising their hands because they had a question. The "i" is easy to form, stands out when hands are raised, and was going to indicate, "I have a question."

The letter "I"
Used to show that the
student has a **question**.

The letter "A"
Used to show that the
student has an **answer**.

Almost immediately after this simple demonstration, I had a student raising his hand to share that his sister knew Signed English, had taught him the alphabet, and maybe we could use the letter "a" to show "I have an answer." Well, I wasn't prepared to do "a" for answer; nonetheless, it's important to share power and decision making with the students. So, we adopted the "a" for answer idea.

We practiced using this new form of hand raising for the next week and saw almost immediate results. I could now clearly see which students had questions and which ones were waiting to share their answers. It enabled me to more effectively meet the needs of the underachievers. (Imagine we had been using this technique during the perimeter review lesson described earlier. After asking the question and looking at the six hands raised, I would have realized that Stephanie had a question. Her "i" sign would have shown me that. And then, aware of the fact that she needed help, I would have calmly halted the lesson and engaged in some reteaching.

MR. MORRIS (SEEING STEPHANIE'S "I" HAND RAISED):
> *Question?*

STEPHANIE:
> *Yeah, Mr. Morris. What's perimeter?*

MR. MORRIS (SMILING PLEASANTLY, OBVIOUSLY PLEASED):
> *Hey, thanks for asking. Would anyone care to answer?*

After a chance for students to respond to Stephanie's question and a quick check to make sure Stephanie was beginning to understand the concept, I could ask the original question again.

MR. MORRIS:
> *All right, thanks for those perimeter explanations. Now then, what's the actual perimeter of this rectangle?*

I bet I would have seen 12-15 hands raised this time. Several students would have had a foggy concept reinforced while many others would have had extra processing time to formulate a response. It would have been a classic win/win situation.

After we had been using "i" and "a" for a few weeks, we realized that there was a category of responses that didn't fit into questions or answers. Sometimes the students just wanted to make a comment of some type. So we added a sign. That's right, it's a "c" for "I have a comment."

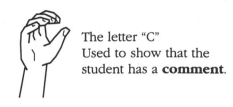

The letter "C"
Used to show that the student has a **comment**.

With three signs to use when a hand is raised, it took a bit of teaching, training, and patience on my part to get them conditioned to this technique. To make it simple and non-verbal, I would merely flash the three different "letters" at any student who was raising a hand that wasn't forming one of the shapes. Within a month, though, it had become second nature to them.

This year I bought a Signed English encyclopedia and added it to our class library. I encouraged the students to look through the book when they had a moment to see if they could find signs we could use in the classroom for communicating. They came up with a bunch of them. (See next page.) And it seemed that they more they learned, the more they wanted to know. In fact, it got to the point whereby I could dismiss them at the end of an assembly by signing directions from across the room.

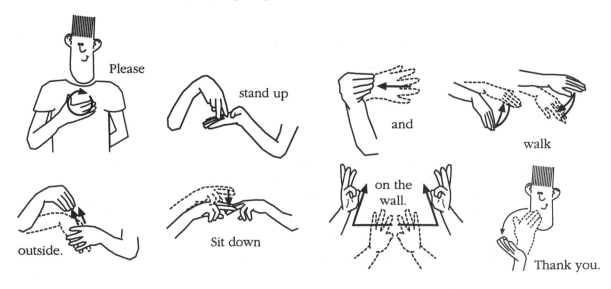

Please stand up and walk outside. Sit down on the wall. Thank you.

One moment, please.

This simple sign, which means "wait a moment," has been extremely useful. It's mainly used for any student who has a comment hand raised while I'm still in the middle of a thought. If I don't acknowledge this student, the hand will stay raised and the student will miss out on what I'm trying to share. By showing this sign, I'm recognizing the fact that the student has a comment to offer yet asking for a moment to finish. After signing and then waiting for the student to lower his hand, I'll complete my thought. When finished I'll get back to the student for his comment.

I also use it to stop someone from interrupting a conversation I'm having with another student. As you know, some students have a tendency to barge into these dialogues without much thought. The sign, which I'll gently place in front of the interrupter's face, allows me to continue my conversation without a needless comment to our meddlesome third party.

Lights off

Lights on

This sign is one I use a lot because our lights are turned off and on at least five or six times a day. I'm either using the overhead projector, reading to them, or just making for an environmental change of pace. Whatever the reason, I'll flash the "lights off" sign to the team that sits near the light switch. One of them will see me and relay the message to the student who actually flips the switch. Using a sign for this repetitive command is far more effective than using my already overused voice. A simple sign and the lights go off. Another sign and they're back on without a single word being said.

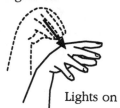

May I use
the restroom?

This is a sign the students use when they wish to use the restroom. It's the letter "r" (crossed fingers) being nodded twice. It's helpful in that I can see this request from across the room and can then nod my head for "yes" or flick my thumb under my chin for "not right now." Either way, the sign prevents students from having to interrupt an activity with a verbal, and sometimes embarrassing, "Can I go to bathroom?"

Line up

So, what do you think? Is Signed English ideal for the classroom, or what? This last one is right up our alley. It's the perfect sign on which to end this mini-encyclopedia because it illustrates the fact that there are a ton of signs that are extremely appropriate for the classroom. Check out a book on signing from you local library, and take it into the room. You'll be amazed at how useful it can be.

Ignoring Someone

For years I've asked my students to ignore bothersome classmates. Ignoring, though, does not satisfy that fundamental human desire to feel powerful and in control. Ignoring is too passive for action-oriented Americans. We like to think that we're taking care of problems, not just overlooking them. So, to help my students become more effective at ignoring rude, interruptive students, I came up with a specific action to go along with the basic ignoring behavior.

The action we use comes from our experience with Signed English. As you discovered on the previous three pages, we use a lot of signs in the classroom to communicate with one another. We expanded our sign language vocabulary by making up a sign which means, "I am ignoring you." (A more accurate definition would probably be, "Listen, Bud. You're buggin' the heck of me. Get outta my face, and leave me alone. I'm tryin' to get some work done here.")

Anyway, the sign is merely a flat hand held between you and the person you are attempting to ignore. Your palm should face toward you. The back of your hand should face toward the person you are attempting to ignore. Be polite when you use this sign. After all, you're not trying to be rude; you're merely showing the person bothering you that you'd rather not be bothered right now.

The "ignorer" knows to come see me if Mr. Bothersome does not get the message. After a quick check to make sure the hand sign and the proper method were used, I'll ask Pest Boy to meet me at the conference center for a brief discussion.

Important factor: Signed English, by its nature, is silent. Therefore, it is difficult to be rude to someone when you are signing, even when the message is, "Leave me alone." Without the signed communication, students are stuck using words which, as we know, have a tendency to get negative.

The Mertilizer

There are many times during the course of the day when it is necessary to get the attention of my students when they are otherwise engaged in some activity. Imagine, for instance, that we've just concluded a spelling lesson and the students are now working independently on the spelling activity sheet. Max, our trusty timer, is keeping track of the time for us. The room has that wonderfully calm atmosphere that sometimes occurs when students are absorbed in completing an assignment. Nevertheless, three minutes into our scheduled fifteen minute work session and a student comes to see me with his paper.

STUDENT (WITH SPELLING ACTIVITY SHEET IN HAND):
>   *Mr. Morris. Something is wrong with sentence #6.*

MR. MORRIS (CHECKING PAPER):
>   *Right you are. That sentence doesn't make any sense. It looks like the printers made a mistake. What do you think you should do?*

STUDENT:
>   *Skip over it?*

MR. MORRIS:
>   *Sounds good to me.*

In the interests of effective management, I should now share this information with everyone else so that I won't have to do it individually as they became aware of the problem with #6. And, since I'll be making a verbal announcement, I should really try to use something other than my voice for alerting the class that an announcement is coming. Otherwise, the words all run together in one, mind-numbing broadcast. To lend significance and impact to my voice—and thus, the message—I decided to use one of the many sound devices we have in class. I grabbed my Mertilizer. (The Mertilizer is a toy space gun that emits a electronic siren kind of sound. I call it the Mertilizer because that's what Calvin calls his ray gun whenever he's in his Spaceman Spiff persona.)

MERTILIZER:
>   *Beep! Beep! Beep!*

MR. MORRIS (WHO NOW HAS THE ATTENTION OF HIS CLASS):
>   *I've just been informed that there is something wrong with #6 on your spelling paper. Check it out.*
> (Pause while students discover that, by golly, he's right.)
>   *You may skip over #6 when you get to it. It just doesn't make sense, and you won't be able to answer it correctly. Thanks.*

And with that, the students get back to the completion of their spelling activity.

Sound devices, from the zany to the musical, work great for alerting your students that you need to tell them something. A quick blast from the Mertilizer, a moment while they look my way, and the message can then be delivered to an attentive audience.

Granted, the whole gun image thing is not the best one to perpetuate in the elementary environment; however, this space toy was the first package I found that contained that wonderful kid-noise. Now, having used sound devices for many years, I've found that they come in a variety of sizes and shapes. In fact, there are so many slick little noise makers out there, we have several different sounds which signal specific actions or commands.

Sound	What it Means
Mertilizer	Stop, look, listen. Used for announcements.
Machine gun	Duck, look, listen. Same as Mertilizer but with a bit of fun thrown in.
Bomb dropping	Have a seat, please.
Train whistle	Line up outside in two, side-by-side rows. (We created our own little imaginary train station outside the room for making this double-line workable.)
Toy accordion	Stand up, please.
Toy telephone	Celebratory signal used during Daily Oral Language.
Hotel bell	Materials are being disseminated. Please send one person from your team to get them.

By using sounds to instruct your students, everyone ends up winning. You cut down on the amount of talking you do, your voice becomes more meaningful, and your students get to exercise their under-used right brains.

SOURCES FOR SOUNDS:
> Check with your students. They can almost always be counted on to have a ready supply of items they'd be willing to loan to the classroom.
> 99¢ Stores. These places can be a gold mine. I've found not only noise makers but all kinds of odds and ends that work in the classroom. And you can't beat the price.
> Garage sales, swap meets, etc.
> Parties. Birthday parties sometimes provide horns while New Year's Eve parties will have clackers.

Cone of Silence

The Cone of Silence is a goofy little toy that the students really seem to enjoy. I don't know whether it has more to do with the fact that it's different or that they get to come to the front of the room and speak to me privately. I'm not sure; I only know it works.

To make your own, you'll need a plastic container of some type. A gallon-sized milk jug will work fine. Get rid of the lid and then remove the label if you can. Next, cut the bottom out of it. That's it.

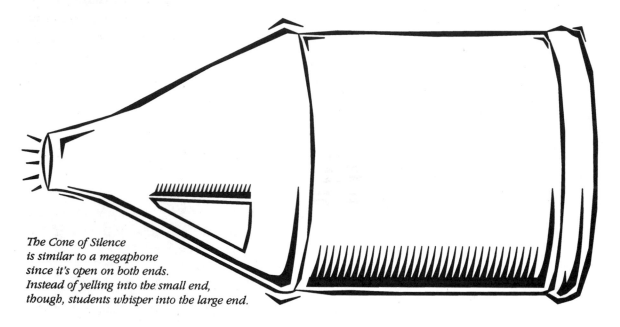

*The Cone of Silence
is similar to a megaphone
since it's open on both ends.
Instead of yelling into the small end,
though, students whisper into the large end.*

The Cone of Silence is used to hear answers from individual students without the others hearing what is being said. All you have to do is place the small end of the cone near your ear with one hand and then indicate with the other hand which students are to come forward.

I use it maybe once a week during a lesson just to give the kids a break from the usual. The Cone of Silence makes for a nice interactive change of pace.

Caution: It doesn't take much volume on the part of the students in order for you to hear their responses. Ask them to speak across the opening of the Cone of Silence and not into it.

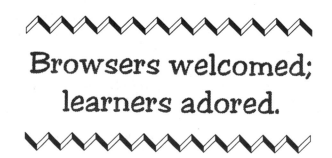

Browsers welcomed;
learners adored.   *Classroom sign*

Overhead Pointer

If you use an overhead projector for teaching, you and your students will love this little toy. It's a pointer that you make from a sheet of overhead transparency film and an old manila file folder.

What you need:

☑ overhead transparency for a copy machine
☑ one manila file folder.

What you do:

1. Make an overhead transparency of this page.
2. Cut around pointing hand artwork.
3. Make a sleeve by cutting off the spine of an old manila file folder. (It should be about 5″X 5/8″.)
4. Slip the sleeve over the arm so that it just covers the black shirt cuff.
5. Staple the sleeve to the arm.

How you use:

Lay it on your overhead, and watch the fun. The visual impact of the arm and see-through hand will capture their attention for what you are trying to highlight.

A high school teacher recently told me how much her students enjoy seeing the hand on their overhead projector. It's even gotten to the point, she said, that if she forgets to use it, the students will ask, "Aren't you going to use Mr. Hand?"

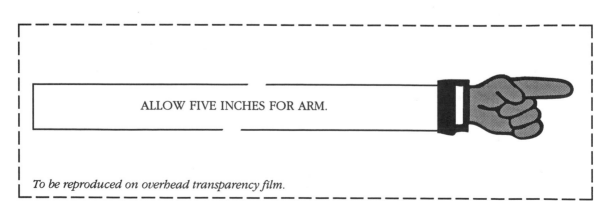

ALLOW FIVE INCHES FOR ARM.

To be reproduced on overhead transparency film.

Dial An Answer

These things are a kick! I think half the fun is saying the name: Dial An Answer! (You'll want to use your best T.V. game show host kind of voice.) This interactive toy is really just a simple way for students to show you what they're thinking—individual assessment if you wish—but with a playful and secretive twist.

What you need:

☑ 36 - 8 ounce paper cups
☑ 1/2" diameter self-adhesive paper dots
☑ a pencil

What you do:

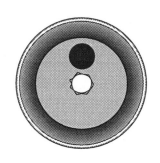

1. With your pencil, punch a hole in the center of the bottom of the cup.
2. On the inside of the cup, between the hole and rim, apply one of the adhesive dots.
3. Hold the cup up to the light so that you are looking at the bottom. You should be able to discern where the adhesive dot is attached to the inside. Using a pencil, write a **1** where you can see the outline of the dot.
4. Turn the cup a quarter turn counter-clockwise, and write a **2**.
5. Turn it again, and write a **3**.
6. Turn it one last time, and write a **4**.

How you use:

Give one to each student. Tell them they will be using their Dial An Answers to show you answers to questions you ask. Let them know there are just two steps to using it.

The first step is to "Dial in your answer." To do this, you spin the cup so that the number you want is at the top, or 12 o'clock position. The second step is to point the open end of the cup toward the teacher and look at her through the hole in the bottom. By doing this, they'll be showing you what they think is the answer. You might want to explain at this point that as they rotate the cup to place their answer at the top, the orange dot on the inside also rotates. By seeing the orange dots on the inside of their cups, you'll know the answers they are selecting.

Sample lesson:

Let's use a basic language exercise. The class has their novels out, and you've directed their attention to page 17. On a piece of scratch paper, have them make a copy of the answer key shown below:

```
1 = noun
2 = verb
3 = adjective
4 = none of the above
```

Now have a student read a sentence from the novel. Choose one of the words from the sentence, and write it on the board.

TEACHER (POINTING TO THE WORD): *What part of speech is this word? Is it a noun, a verb, an adjective, or none of these? Dial in your answer.*

As the students make a choice and and look at you through the hole in bottom of the cup—which is entertaining in itself—you will see the dots in a variety of positions. Those positions, and the answers they represent, will look like this:

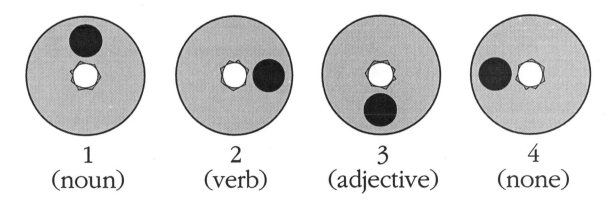

| 1 | 2 | 3 | 4 |
| (noun) | (verb) | (adjective) | (none) |

The immediate—and, for the most part, genuine—feedback you receive from your students as they respond will help you direct your lessons. You'll know when to reteach and when to move on. The simple pleasure of watching your students use this classroom toy is an added bonus not to be missed.

When we're finished using them for the day, they're collected by team, stacked up, and set aside until the next time we need them.

Opportunity: As most of you have realized, you can certainly use these for reciprocal teaching situations. I would imagine that a student would love to have all of those cups pointed in his direction. A little bit of power and a whole lot of fun.

Stretching Exercises: How about using the Dial An Answer as a team thing? You could pose your questions to the teams who would then be able to conference. After a team had reached a decision, one of the team members could stand and show you their answer.

Counseling Center

Blackline master in appendix

We have a double desk set aside in our room for students who need to take a "time out" due to their negative behavior or poor attitude. It's just one of the interventions I use so that I can focus on positive behavior. By having the Counseling Center in the room, I can maintain a professional, hands-on supervision of even my most disruptive students.

In the past I had these students wait outside for me. Outside didn't work well. There's no supervision, there's lost contact with the lesson being conducted, the student lost face, and, at some point in time, I had to step out of the room to deal with the child. In-room is better.

Let's say, for whatever reason, Calvin's being a coconut. We're trying to deal with a plant life activity and he's acting out some scene from *The Bad Seed*.

> MR. MORRIS (CALM YET FIRM):
>
> *Calvin. Would you please take a seat
> at the Counseling Center? Thanks.*

And I'm right back to my science lesson. Calvin gets up from his seat, heads over to the Counseling Center, and reads the directions on the stand-up sign we have on display.

Now that I have Calvin removed from his regularly assigned seat and have him safely ensconced in an alternate study area *(see bottom of page 35)* I'll need to go see him ASAP. At some time during the next five minutes, I will generate some type of two-minute individual or team-based activity which briefly reviews or summarizes what we've just covered.

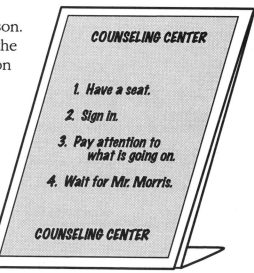

> MR. MORRIS:
>
> *Take two minutes, talk to your team, and decide what the
> three key ingredients are for plant growth. List your three
> elements on a team card, and place it on the podium, please.*

And with that, I'm off to the Counseling Center to see my desperately needy little buddy, Calvin. As you can imagine, I won't have a great deal of time with which to interact with him. My main concern is to reinforce the fact that he took care of his Counseling Center agenda in a reasonable manner, i.e., he sat down, he signed in (see FIGURE 56.1), and he paid attention to the science lesson that had continued during his time of personal trauma.

MR. MORRIS (CHECKING THE SIGN-IN LOG):

> *I see you signed in. Thanks. Now then, what seems to be the problem?*

CALVIN:

> *Jason's bothering me. He keeps teasing me about my new haircut.*

It is usually a case wherein someone is bothering him or causing him to act in an inappropriate fashion. Sometimes he's so worked up he can't even speak. (That's why the sign-in sheet only asks for a name, a student number, and a date. Most kids going to the C.C. are so agitated that they couldn't put down any coherent reason for their presence.) What I need to show Calvin is that I'm concerned; however, we only have a limited amount of time for dialoguing his current crisis and identifying possible solutions or corrective actions.

MR. MORRIS:

> *I'm sorry to hear that, but we need to get back to our lesson, bud. Why don't we talk about it later? I'd be happy to see you at recess or after school.*

This statement does wonders for my "socially challenged" students. The message they receive is something along these lines:

> *Mr. Morris cares.*
> *Mr. Morris wants to help.*
> *Mr. Morris is willing to listen.*

After this brief interaction, Calvin is sent back to his seat to rejoin his team and the lesson. (If it would help Calvin engage in the lesson or if he simply needs more time to cool off, I'd ask if he'd like to stay at the C.C. for the remainder of the lesson. He would then see this space as a workable alternative to suffering at his seat. We're always trying to turn negatives into positives.)

Counseling Center, Act II

If Calvin were to act inappropriately after being sent to the Counseling Center, I would most likely send him from the room for a time-out period. After setting Max for fifteen minutes, I'd walk Calvin to the door and point to the room next to us. (I have a reciprocal arrangement with one of my neighbors.) Calvin would then go next door and sit in the time-out chair. At the end of the time, Max will beep. One of our students will go get Calvin and bring him back to our room. These interventions, Counseling Center and Time Out, are just two of the many we use. As you know, the more interventions you have, the more effective you'll be at meeting the needs of your students.

Counseling Center Log:

Sitting on the desk that forms the Counseling Center is a folder which contains the sign-in sheets. The sheets look like this:

Counseling Center Log

Name/#	Date	SB
Calvin #17	9/10	
Jennifer #20	Sept. 10	
Calvin #17	Sept. 12	╱

FIGURE 56.1

The box marked "SB" is for Student Bulletins. (See page 32.) Since Calvin has been to the Counseling Center twice in three days, it seemed appropriate to apprise his parents of this. When I met with him, I had him fill out a SB. I then drew a diagonal line through the box on the C. C. log as a reminder that he has taken a bulletin home to his parents. When he returns it, I'll draw a second diagonal line which will form an X.

The folder is a simple Two-Pocket Portfolio with Grommets. (If you look for them in the office supply store near you, that's how they'll be labeled.) The pockets are handy for holding loose papers and notes while the grommets allow you to insert your own forms that have been 3-hole punched. It's also a good idea to have a cup of pencils available at the Counseling Center. This will save Calvin a trip back to seat to find a writing tool so that he can sign in.

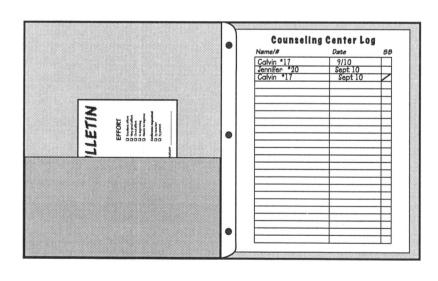

And again, we're not looking for some detailed description as to why these students are being sent to the Counseling Center. I just want some simple documentation as to who's been visiting and when. Name, number, and date will be sufficient.

Extension: Buy yourself an inexpensive, stick-on digital clock (check in the auto/hardware section of a discount drug store) and attach it to a wall or cabinet near your counseling center. As a form of intervention, you could send a student to the center to "take two" as in minutes. No sign-in necessary; just a self-regulated two-minute time-out, and then it's back to business as usual.

Name Tag Signs

Here's a fun way to communicate with your students without having to rely upon your voice.

1. Get yourself a simple name tag holder. (Check with your secretary before you go to the stationery store. Some schools use these for their visitors.)

2. Cut some bright construction paper to the proper size. Keep a supply on hand.

Sample name tag sign (Book Report?) being worn as a non-verbal reminder to students that a book report is due later in the day.

3. Write your message, and insert it in the name tag holder.

4. Wear it but don't announce it. Let them make the discovery.

How's your packet?

Spelling Test 10:30

Vocabulary: PLURALISM

Are you ready for a desk inspection?

It's A Funny Business: I had the best reaction to a sign I wore for my third graders one year. It simply said: "Don't read this sign." Of course you have to read it to know this and then it's too late. Thinking about their puzzled expressions as they valiantly tried to figure it all out still brings a smile to my face.

Record Keepers

Excerpted from the book, "Class Cards: A New Management Teaching Tool"

This handy little tool is a simple, yet effective, variation on the basic Class Cards idea. Since these cards will be made from 3 X 5 index cards, you'll be able to write on them for purposes of documentation. By using these new Class Cards during specific lessons, you will have the ability to keep a basic record of how well your students are responding and participating in these subjects.

What you need:

☑ set of 3 X 5 plain index cards
    (one per student)
☑ fine point permanent ink felt tip pen
☑ class roster

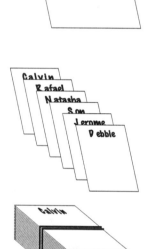

What you do:

1. Write the name of a student at the top of a card.
2. Keep making cards until you've made a card for each student.
3. Hold them together with a clip or rubber band.

How you use:

Use these cards the way you would a regular set of Class Cards; i.e., call upon students to respond based upon the card on the top of the deck. The difference, of course, is that you can actually keep track of the responses[†] by marking a + or a – on these cards.

It's absolutely amazing to see how attentive students become when they realize that their responses are being immediately documented.

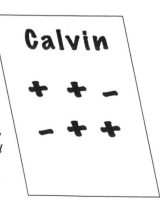

Calvin's card with positive and negative responses marked. Since these cards are purely objective in the manner that they show student performance, I find myself surprised by how well my Calvins are sometimes doing. Record Keepers help me to more fairly acknowledge their achievement.

† Responses, both positive and negative, are not always specific answers to specific questions. Imagine, for example, that the class is reading orally from the textbook. If a student, when called on to read, begins promptly, a + would be recorded. Conversely, a student who is not following the lesson and does not know where to begin reading when called on would receive a – mark on his card. Response opportunities can be as varied as the teaching strategies being employed.

Record Keepers can be a great way to motivate your students with difficult subjects. Although it will take a number of days to get the message across, a set of Record Keepers is a great way to start. Let's use an example a friend of mine shared with me recently.

She was experiencing some difficulty with her fourth graders during their daily health lesson. This lesson was the last one before lunch, and she felt that their attention was lagging and needed a boost of some sort. Her solution? A set of Record Keepers just for health. (She used green index cards for this set so that it would stand out.)

For the day's health lesson, she used her new set of cards. She called on each student once, and recorded their responses. She also placed the cards in two piles: positive responses and negative responses. By the end of the lesson, everyone had had an opportunity to respond in some way.

To dismiss them for lunch, she first picked up the + pile. These students were identified and sent to lunch. The remaining group of students, the ones who had received a – for their responses, were in need of some type of motivation. Her dialogue might have gone something like this:

TEACHER (LOOKING THROUGH THE – CARDS.):
For some reason you boys and girls were not staying with today's health lesson. Now, I know for a fact that the health assignment for today was on the board this morning.
(Pointing to page numbers on the chalkboard…)
And that the vocabulary words for today were listed. And I seem to remember bringing this to everyone's attention this morning with the suggestion that you look it over if you had any free time. Now then, are we going to be learning about health tomorrow?

(Lots of head nodding.)

TEACHER:
Right you are. Will I be using this deck of cards
(waving green health cards in front of group)
to call on students?

(More head nodding.)

TEACHER:
Right again. You wouldn't want to end up with two minus marks in a row, if you know what I mean. Please stay with the lesson tomorrow. Any questions? Enjoy your lunch.

Regardless of what was actually said to these students, they were made to understand that the teacher was aware of, and concerned about, their daily progress. This important realization on the part of the students can be a key motivational factor.

Xeroxable Record Keepers

Writing the names of your students on index cards is just one way you can make a set of Record Keepers. For you hardcore efficiency types, there is another method.

What you need:

- ☑ permanent ink felt tip pen
- ☑ 4-5 sheets of ditto paper
- ☑ a neighborhood Kinko's or similiar copy shop

What to do:

1. Fold the paper into eighths. Unfold.
2. Write the names of eight students on one sheet.
3. Keep writing names until you have them all on paper.
4. Take the sheets to Kinko's, and have them make copies on card stock. (Card stock is a type of heavy paper. It comes in a variety of colors.)
5. On the paper cutter, chop the copies so that you end up with a set of cards.
6. File your originals until you need them again.

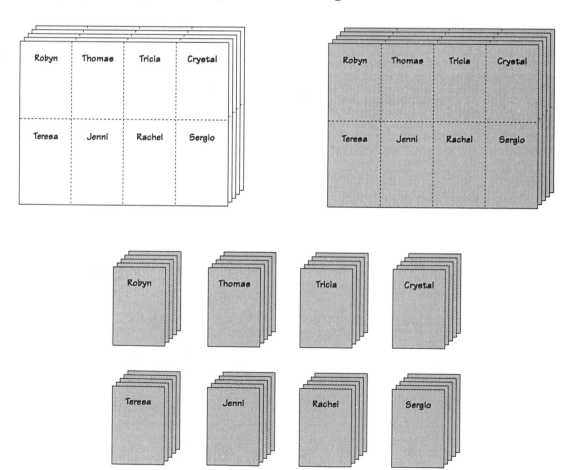

Suggestion: As long as you're at Kinko's making a set, have them run off a set or two in different colors. (They have 16.) Before you know it, you'll have figured out some clever way to use those other sets.

Report Cards
Using cards you can mark on will provide you with a record of each student's effort in one particular subject. Along with the muscle they'll add to your daily interactions, a deck of Record Keepers will act as a handy reference guide at report card time.

Reward Deck
After using a set of Record Keepers for a unit of study, give the deck to a student. The student will then check each card. The pluses are counted, and the total is written in felt pen on the card. Cards can then given back to students to spend on snacks or privileges.

Hat Trick
With certain decks of Record Keepers, I'll reward students with a coupon for every third plus. (When an ice hockey player scores three goals in a game they call it a hat trick.) On the third plus, I'll say, "Hat trick." As the lesson continues, the hat tricker comes forward for his coupon.

SILENT ANSWERS

To give underachievers more time to formulate a response, I'll take silent answers from those students who appear to be ready.

MR. MORRIS:
> *Silent answers, please.*

Students who wish to respond will raise an answer hand. *(See Signed English, page 43.)* As I point to a student, he will mouth the answer, and I'll lipread it. A nod, a wink, or a smile will let them know that the response was correct. After taking a number of these silent answers, I'll then call upon the student whose card is on top of the deck of Record Keepers for an oral response.

Aside from the entertainment value of watching my students as they attempt to mouth the words, taking silent answers has proven to be a very effective method for maintaining total class involvement while providing more processing time for my underachievers.

Red Hands

Blackline master in appendix

If you've taught for more than a week, then you already know how annoying it is to be in the middle of a question/answer session with your students only to have one of them blurt out an answer. It's a real drag on you and the other students to remind someone over and over again to raise a hand before responding.

Well, remind no more. With this little paper tool you'll be able to act upon your expectations of behavior and not just talk about them.

Red Hands are cut from red construction paper using an Ellison die cutter. They are kept on my desk. Whenever a student blurts out an answer or response when it is inappropriate to do so, I stop everything, pick up one of the Red Hands, and extend it to the blurter. He is then required to go over to the Counseling Center where he writes his name and the date on the hand. The hand is then dropped into a plastic container that "holds hands."

At the end of the week, a student goes through the container and records the hands on a grade sheet. The students with the most Red Hands have them stapled to a Red Hand bulletin *(see appendix)* which is then sent home. It's this type of specific, goal-oriented communication that really gets results. We're not saying that Calvin is hopelessly irresponsible; it's just that he needs to exercise a bit more self-control.

Recommended: At the end of the week, you could recognize or reward everyone who did not have any hands in the container. This will encourage them to continue to abide by your classroom rules.

The Red Hands Calvin received during the week are eventually stapled to a Red Hand bulletin and sent home. The visual impact of these cutout hands helps to highlight Calvin's need for self-control.

Repeating An Answer

Excerpted from the book, "Class Cards: A New Management Teaching Tool"

This interactive technique will help to encourage positive listening on the part of your students. Students need to understand that the teacher is not the only source of wisdom. Other students can often be fountains of knowledge during discussions. Unfortunately, they usually don't pay attention to one another. They're either focused on you, themselves, or nothing at all. So, to help reinforce the fine art of positive listening, I'll call upon someone to repeat a response just given by a student.

In the beginning we heard a lot of "I didn't hear what he said." In fact, we heard it so often that we decided to do something about it.

Our decision was:

When you can't hear someone, raise your hand and say that person's name.

The person who had just spoken will then repeat his answer more clearly.

It's a simple procedure which reinforces the concept of students being responsible for their own education. (It is also beneficial for the soft-spoken members of your class who need to improve their oral language skills.) Now that students will no longer be able to rely upon the time-honored phrase, "I didn't hear what he said," they'll be more attentive listeners.

Reality: If I'm a student in class and I didn't clearly hear what Jason just said, I'm going to raise my hand and say, "Jason." I never know when Mr. Morris is going to ask me to repeat Jason's bit of wisdom.

Caution: Getting students to the point where they'll ask for repeat answers on their own is a bit of a process. You'll first have to overcome the urge to ditch the whole thing when, after introducing this idea, you'll hear just about everyone screaming out the names of other students. So, allow time for the novelty factor to work itself out. Then, develop the habit of calling upon students to repeat something that was just said by one the students. This can be done in a variety of ways. Sometimes when a student has just offered a rather soft oral response that I know some of the students didn't hear, I'll look toward the group and say, "Man, you guys back there must have some good ears." The hands go up and the name comes out. Nurturing of this sort is just part of being an effective teacher.

Part IV
Number Tools

Art Hangers

There never seems to be enough space in the classroom to lay art projects, especially art that needs to dry. Tabletops, counters, and desks will only be able to handle so many papers. Besides, stacking wet paintings or block prints one upon another will produce less than desired results.

Our solution was to install a retractable clothesline (about $15 in your local hardware store) and provide a set of numbered clothespins. When needed, the clothesline is extended. Students then clip their art work to the line with their clothespins. At the end of the day, the artwork is then ready to be saved for permanent display in the room or distributed to be taken home.

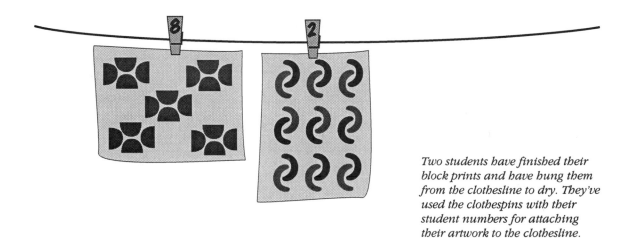

Two students have finished their block prints and have hung them from the clothesline to dry. They've used the clothespins with their student numbers for attaching their artwork to the clothesline.

Bonus: Many students get so caught up in the art process that they forget to put their names on their piece. Writing your name on a finished, but still wet painting is difficult at best. By using a numbered clothespin to hang the art, a name is not really necessary for identification. The number on the clothespin will suffice until such time as the work of art dries and the artist signs his name.

Suggestion: An old, floppy hat makes a great clothespin holder. You can hang it on the wall, clothespins attached like so many legs on a centipede, until you need to take it down for the students to use.

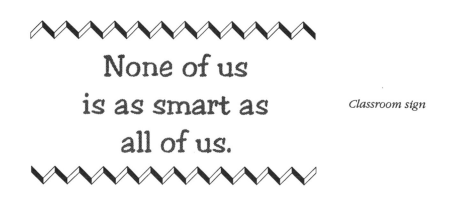

None of us
is as smart as
all of us.

Classroom sign

Roll-A-Matic

The Roll-A-Matic is an attendance taking device. It is simply a piece of pegboard that holds golf tees. Before the students come to school, the golf tees are in the first row. Then, as students enter the room, they move the golf tees one hole to the right. This not only lets me know who is here for the day but also allows the students to exercise responsibility. They're not two steps in the door and already they're taking care of business.

Obviously this technique will present a bit of difficulty if your students all enter the room at the same time. (My guys come in over the course of thirty minutes or so.) If that's the case, see what you can do to make it work. The important part is not expedience, it's giving your students practice at being responsible. Granted you could conduct the entire roll process yourself; nonetheless, that's just another example of teacher welfare. Break the mold; set 'em free.

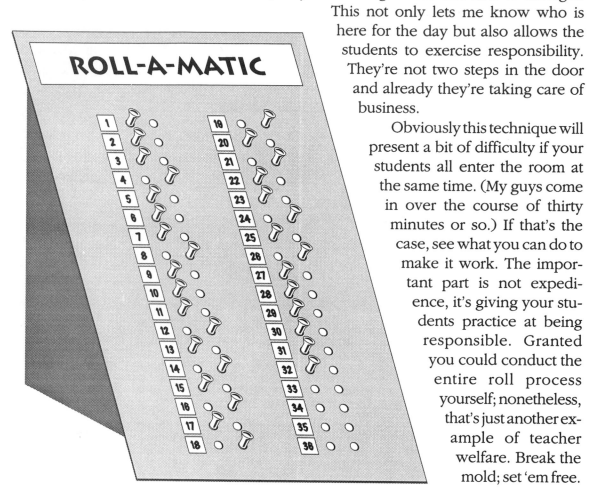

Students 4, 8, 12, 14, 16, 18, 19, 21, 24, and 26 have checked in by moving their golf tees to the second row.

Suggestion: You might want to put a student in charge. After the morning bell rings, this student will see who is at school and who is not. He can then let the teacher know. After the absent students have been marked in the attendance folder, the student manager can move the tees back to the first row.

Extension: I heard a student teacher at San Diego State University describe an attendance taking tool her master teacher had made. It was a parking garage made from a cardboard box. She used a felt pen and created parking spaces complete with the names of her students. Next to the garage she placed a basket of small toy cars and trucks. As students entered the room, they chose vehicles and placed them in their parking spaces. They also had a student parking attendant who would check to see who hadn't made it to class that day. Cool idea. The only problem I can see is that the structure so lovingly crafted will become obsolete the next year as the students move on and new ones enter. If, however, the spaces had been numbered instead of named, the parking garage would be ready for the next group on the first day of the new school year. You just can't beat those numbers for making life easier.

Number Stickers

Here's a great way to help students keep track of their books and supplies. We call 'em Number Stickers.

What you need:

☑ 1/2″ diameter self-adhesive circles
☑ permanent ink felt tip pen
☑ scissors

What you do:

1. Using the permanent marker, make a set of number stickers for each student.
2. Cut the sheets of circles into strips.
3. Give each student his set of numbered stickers.
4. Have students apply them to the front cover of each book.
5. Place extra stickers in Tool Kits.

Adding a number sticker to the front cover helps in a number of ways. First, students will have an easier time of managing their sets of textbooks. The numbers make sorting and organizing a snap. Also, when a book has been left out, anyone in class will be able to return it to the owner without undo hassle. Finally, when it's time to collect books, you'll be able to confidently check off each student as they return the original book issued.

Other stickerable items:
> pencil box   > crayon box   > calculators
> back of ruler   > personal clipboard   > whatever

Recommended: If you receive sets of novels from your central media center, it might make more sense to use a permanent ink, fine point felt marker and number each book in your set. (The inside back cover is an effective yet discrete location for the numbers.) Since number stickers can be peeled off, students might be inclined to "borrow" another student's book to replace the one they've lost. Permanent numbers would prevent this from happening, protecting the innocent and responsible alike.

Clip 'Em, Dano

There are times when:

1)   everyone has just completed a simple assignment and
2)   I want to collect them quickly.

Bell Math, a four-minute math drill done immediately after the morning bell rings would be a good example of this type of activity. After solving the problems, exchanging papers, and then correcting them, I want to collect them.

MR. MORRIS:
Okay. Let's Clip 'Em!

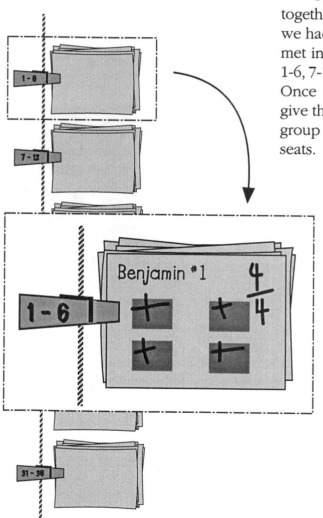

Students grab their papers and get together in student number groups. (Since we had thirty-six students last year, they met in groups of six. The groups were: 1-6, 7-12, 13-18, 19-24, 25-30, and 31-36.) Once a group is together, the students give their Bell Math papers to one of the group members and then return to their seats.

The student with the six papers collates them and walks over to the Clip 'Em, Dano clothespins. He then clips all six papers to the appropriate clothespin and sits down. Within a minute or so, all six groups will have met, the papers will have been gathered, collated, and clipped. Later on, a student clerk will walk over to the clothespins and unclip the groups of papers from the top group (1-6) to the bottom group (31-36) and place them in the To Be Recorded tote tray.

Reality: After doing this for just a bit, the different groups will each develop their own technique for gathering papers. Some groups will continue to meet while others will have one of the members make "house calls" on the others. As you know, it doesn't really matter as long as we're takin' care of business in a timely fashion.

Collating Folders

Here's another collection/collation device for handling assignments. It's made of manila folders stapled together and numbered. Not only is it simple to make, but the materials can be found in your school's supply room.

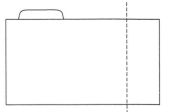

What you need:

- ☑ 36 manila file folders
- ☑ stapler
- ☑ permanent marker
- ☑ paper cutter

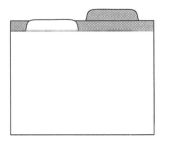

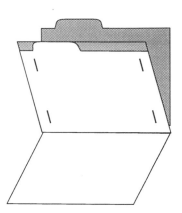

What you do:

1. Cut the manila folders so that they are 8″ wide. Make sure you cut the end that doesn't have the label tab.
2. Take two folders and lay one on top of the other so that the tabs are on the same side. Align the folders so that the top edge of the tab on folder 1 lines up with the top front edge of folder 2.
3. Staple the back of folder 1 to the front of folder 2.
4. Keep adding folders to the top until you end up with 36 folders.
5. Using your permanent marker, number the tabs from 1 to 36.

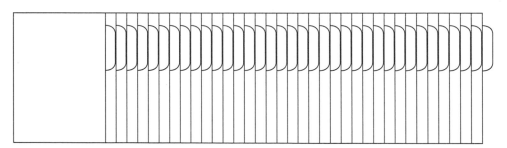

How you use:

Place fingers on numbered tab, lift cover, and insert paper. Sounds simple, but be prepared for a week or two of learning as the students, at their own speeds, figure out the proper process for getting their papers in the proper places. Even though you'll explain it carefully and might even demo the idea yourself, it's going to be one of those "learn by living" things. Be patient.

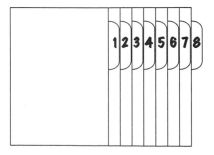

Did you figure out why we cut the folders before assembling the collator? That's right. The papers will stick out top and bottom making them easier to extract.

Manila Envelope Check Off List

Here's a slick little variation on the basic Check Off List. It was created by one of my former students[†]. I had given her a COL because she was going to be collecting the permission slips for a field trip we were planning. I had also given her a manila envelope for holding the forms as she processed them.

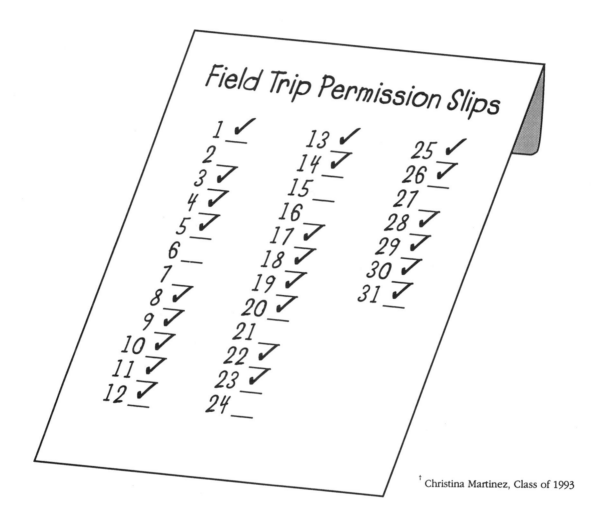

[†] Christina Martinez, Class of 1993

Well, she came back later in the day and returned the unused COL. She told me she wasn't going to need it after all. She had written her own Check Off List on the front of the manila envelope! What a great idea.

It is a source of never-ending joy and surprise to see my students coming up with their own variations on the ideas we are using in the classroom. It also reinforces the "None of us is as smart as all of us" concept.

Stretching exercises: Maybe you could send an envelope around the room as a way to collect something. As students receive the envelope, they would insert the required item and mark off their numbers.

Islands

Blackline master in appendix

Islands are tote trays that do more than hold broken crayons or the leftover copies of last year's Weekly Reader. With the addition of a clipboard and a Check Off Sheet, they help take care of assignment collection.

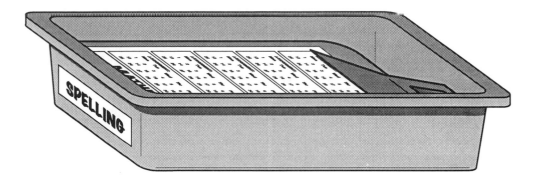

Here's how our spelling island works:

1. The spelling assignment for the day is given to the students.
2. Leftover assignment sheets are placed in the bottom of the island or the Extra Papers tote tray. *(See Extra Papers, page 4)*
3. I then pick up the clipboard that holds the spelling Check Off Sheet and fill in the necessary information. The clipboard is then placed in the island.
4. The island is now set in some convenient, easy-to-get-to location.
5. As students complete the assignment, they place it under the clipboard and mark off their numbers.
6. I'll take the island with me at the end of the day for processing. Since everything I need is in one place, it becomes easier to handle.

On the clipboard, top to bottom:

- Check Off Sheet being used
- Extra Check Off Sheet
- Check Off Sheet blackline master

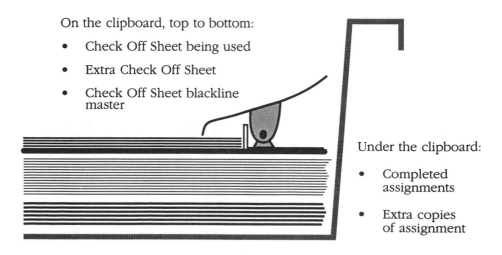

Under the clipboard:

- Completed assignments
- Extra copies of assignment

Opportunity: Keeping a grade sheet under the Check Off Sheet on your clipboard would allow for immediate recording of scores or grades.

Clothespin Check Off List

The opportunities for using a Check Off List for collecting assignments should not be limited to a flat, static, two-dimensional piece of paper. Although the paper model works quite well, there is a host of alternative media available.

One of the best is a set of numbered clothespins and a cardboard box. These wooden pins, numbered on both sides of the open end, are placed around the lip of the box. As a student places an assignment in the box, he removes his clothespin, and puts it in a small container that sits next to the box. Just like the original paper COL, you'll be able to see who is finished and who is not.

There are two advantages to using manipulatives for collection tools. One is that it's more fun for the students. Another is that you will need a student (involvement) to reset the tool for you so that it is ready for the next day.

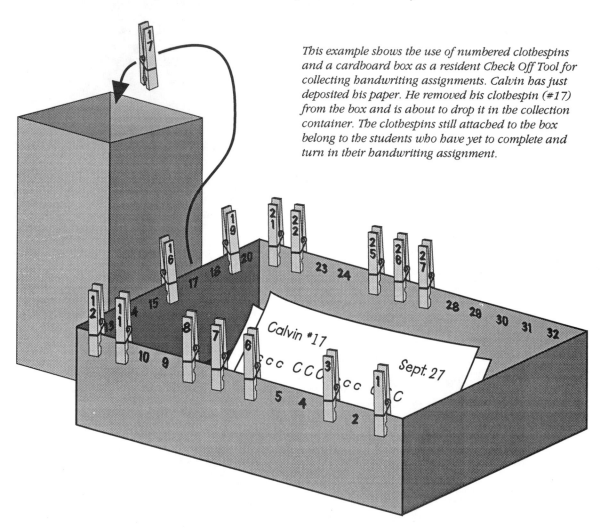

This example shows the use of numbered clothespins and a cardboard box as a resident Check Off Tool for collecting handwriting assignments. Calvin has just deposited his paper. He removed his clothespin (#17) from the box and is about to drop it in the collection container. The clothespins still attached to the box belong to the students who have yet to complete and turn in their handwriting assignment.

Bonus: Maybe, as you walk by the Clothespin COL, you could randomly select a clothespin from the container. The student whose clothespin you pulled could be given a coupon for a drawing or some other reward. This will reinforce that most basic of all work skills: completing assignments on time.

Teacher/Student Agreements

Blackline master in appendix

In an effort to both decrease the amount of reminding I have to do and increase the level of accountability on the part of my students, I instituted a pseudo-legal agreement binder and began to fill it with Teacher/Student Agreements (TSA's.)

A TSA is a standardized form which describes a rule or specifies some type of expected behavior. At the bottom of the form are spaces for students to sign their initials indicating their commitment to abide by the stated agreement. Completed TSA's are kept in a 3-ring binder. It's the perfect reference tool for dealing with anyone who might try to say, "I didn't know."

To begin this system, I'll xerox approximately 10 copies of the basic TSA form, 3-hole punch them, and then place them in the binder. I'll then write the first agreement on the top form. (It's usually the one about textbooks.) This agreement is then read to the class. After a brief discussion, the TSA is placed on a clipboard and left in a convenient location. When

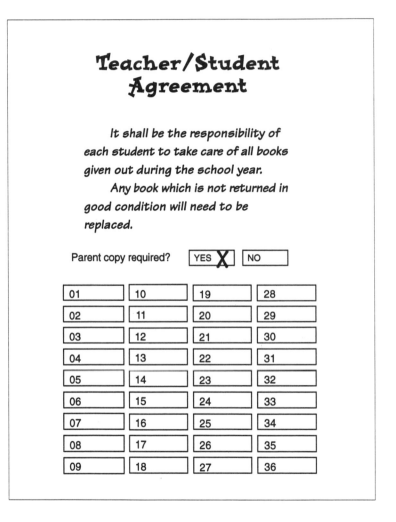

students have time during the course of the day, they sign their initials in the proper boxes. (A reminder to sign the TSA might be a good header for the E.T. Chart.) After everyone has had a chance to sign the form, it is then returned to the binder. The Teacher/Student Agreement binder is usually kept at the Counseling Center.

Parent Copy Required? There are certain agreements which I feel should be shared with the parents. When that is the case, I'll check the YES box below the statement. Students are then required to make a copy of the agreement and have it signed by their parents. (Make an overhead or have a student write the agreement on the board for your class to copy.) As students bring back their signed copies, draw a line through their students numbers. This will keep you apprised of their progress at returning them.

Part V
Team Tools

Rainbow Cards

There are many times during the course of the week when we need the teams to take turns doing something. It might be something as routine as turning in an assignment by team or reading written work in front of the other students. It could also be something a bit more meaningful to them: visiting the classroom snack shop or heading to the library. If I perform some kind of arbitrary pick-and-choose to establish the order, I'm setting myself up for failure.

B.R.C. (Before Rainbow Cards)

> MR. MORRIS (LOOKING AROUND THE ROOM AT THE TEAMS):
> > *Okay, let's see which team is ready to choose their art materials*
> > *for today's special project.*
> > (Students scramble trying to appear ready.)
> > *How......about......the.........Green Team!*
> > (Sounds of glee from the Greenies; sounds of derision, despair,
> > and frustration from the others.)

What I've learned to do in these situations is use our Rainbow Cards. These cards, one per team, determine the order. It's simple. It's fair. It's even somewhat dramatic.

A.R.C. (After Rainbow Cards)

> MR. MORRIS (SHUFFLING THE SIX RAINBOW CARDS):
> > *We need to send teams back to the conference tables so that*
> > *they can get their art supplies for the project. While you're*
> > *waiting for your turn, you can clear your desks and get out a*
> > *pair of scissors.*

With that, I turn to the wall behind my desk and hang the Rainbow Cards from the six nails. (I usually hang cards from right to left so that we have a bit of suspense as to which team will be first.) The students can then see the order in which they will be getting supplies.

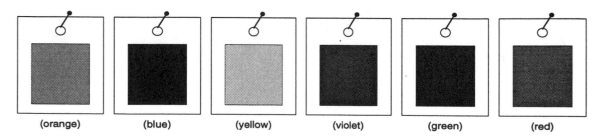

| (orange) | (blue) | (yellow) | (violet) | (green) | (red) |

Rainbow cards are made by gluing colored rectangles to 4 X 6 index cards. The cards are then laminated and punched. You'll also need nails or hooks from which to hang them.

Rainbow Order Reward: We have a standing bet in Room 12. If the cards end up in rainbow order (ROYGBV) they get extra recess. Even though the odds of this happening are slim—I've yet to see it in the six years I've been using these cards—they still faithfully await the moment it's going to appear.

Materials Place Mat

This easy-to-make tool helps me to more effectively get materials and supplies to the six teams of students. It also acts as an exercise for reinforcing cooperation and responsibility as team members.

What you need:

- ☑ 6 sheets of 9″X 12″ construction paper (red, orange, yellow, green, blue, violet)
- ☑ scotch tape

What you do:

1. Take the sheets of construction paper and lay them side-by-side in rainbow order. Leave a slight gap between each sheet.
2. Tape the sheets together.
3. Turn the sheets over, and tape the back side.

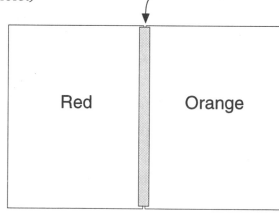

How you use:

Place your mat on a table or bookcase. Put the necessary materials on each sheet. Announce that there are materials each team needs to get. (You might want to use a special sound maker as a "come get materials" signal.) The teams will then select one student to go forward and pick up what you've placed on their colored sheet of paper.

The advantages to using this place mat are that 1) it provides a central place for me to disseminate materials and teams to collect them and 2) I can quickly tell which team does not yet have the supplies it needs.

Bonus: Sometimes teams will inadvertently send up two students to get the same thing. By using a place mat, you'll prevent any team from receiving more than they really need. The second student would find an empty sheet of paper and would, it is hoped, head back to his team to find out what's up. If he asked me about the missing materials, I'd ask him to check with his team.

Team Cards

Whenever it's appropriate, I like to have the teams make decisions affecting the course of events. In order to make the best use of team discussion time and to help them bring their discussion to closure, we ask that they write their final decision on a team card and submit it to me. Team cards are pieces of pre-cut note paper approximately 3″ X 6″ in size. Each team has a ready supply of them along with a Crayola watercolor marker in its team color.

What they do:
1. The team reaches a decision. (Allow 2-3 days for this part.)
2. Their decision is then written on a team card.
3. Using their felt pen, a line—a swoosh, if you will—is drawn across the top.
4. The team card is then delivered to the front of the room where it is laid on top of the podium from which I operate.
5. After all team cards have been submitted, a final decision is announced to the class.

By basing our actual choice upon the decisions written on the team cards, the students eventually realize that they are powerful decision makers. And, for the sake of expedience, we don't have to spend any unnecessary time polling each team for its decision. A quick look at the team cards gives me all the info we need.

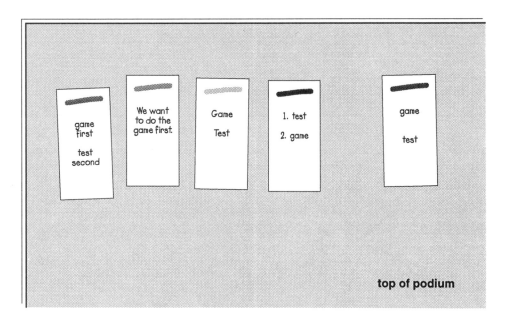

In the example above, student teams were deciding which activity to do first: a math test or a math game. The illustration shows team cards being laid out on the podium. I usually keep them in rainbow order. The color swooshes—made with a Crayola marker—make it easy to identify teams. As you can see, we were still waiting for the blue team to submit its vote on whether we should take the math test first or play the math game first. After all cards had been received, their decision—game first, test second—was announced.

Glossary

activity sheet is the term we use for work sheets. Activity or learning has a more positive slant than "work" does.

alternate study areas are places where students can relocate themselves for studying, reading, or completing assignments. We use our Counseling Center, the conference tables, and an outside desk for alternate study areas.

Calvin is the name I use for my generic problem child. Calvin is the main character of a comic strip created by Bill Waterson. Feel free to substitute your favorite name whenever you see Calvin mentioned in the book.

COL is an abbreviation for Check Off List. The Check Off List is a student number tool that is used for recording the completion of tasks. Although it is a paper form in its basic state, there are simple variations you can create.

Roll-A-Matic	page 68
Manila Envelope COL	page 72
Clothespin COL	page 74

Max is the name of our Westbend® digital timer. Even though it wasn't included in this book, digital timers are fabulous tools for keeping track of time frames. Not only does Max's beeping sound announce the end of the work period, it also acts as a stress reducer. I no longer have to worry about keeping part of my awareness on how much time is left before we need to move on to something else. I just set the time, announce it to the students, get Max started, and then forget about it. All of my energy goes toward the students and their needs. Max takes care of the tedious time-tracking tasks. It's been the best money I've spent in my twenty years of teaching.

pod is the name we use for the group of desks a team uses. The standard formation, created from three double-desks looks something like this:

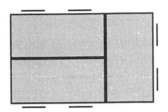

staff meeting is the term we use for class meeting. Since we normally talk about administrative things—turning in forms for the office, collecting permission slips, announcing assemblies or meetings—I felt that staff meeting had a better ring to it. As Thoreau stated: "Language is a volatile truth." Call your five minutes of info sharing a staff meeting and it sounds rather significant.

teams are groups of students who work together at a pod throughout the year. We have six teams and identify them with rainbow colors: red, orange, yellow, green, blue, and violet. (It's not purple because the colors come from the light spectrum; hence, ultra-violet instead of ultra-purple.) The teams can be great sources of information and support. (If you're not sure about something, you can always check with your team. Someone will help you find the answer.) This is not to say that we are constantly working in a cooperative fashion. Actually, the norm is more along the lines of "working alone together." It's just nice having people you've come to trust there for you when you need them.

Note: When forming teams, find and place an "encourager" on each team before anyone else. This person, regardless of academic ability, will keep everyone else moving when things reach an impasse.

Appendix
of
Blackline
Masters

Guide to Blackline Masters

Check Off List (COL):

Use for collecting assignments. Mark off student numbers as assignments are handed in. You might want to pencil in the names of your students next to the numbers before making the xerox copies. This will make it easier to remember which number is associated with which student.

Check Off Sheet:

Similar to a Check Off List in that it is used for collecting and tracking completed assignments. The advantage to the sheet is that it retains a record of how students are doing in a particular subject day after day. For instance, if I use a set of sheets to collect the 20 assignments we'll complete for a chapter in math, I'll end up with some useful documentation of the effort students had given. Individual Check Off Lists don't offer this tracking advantage. (See Islands, page 73.)

Mini Grade Sheet:

Use for recording grades. These forms are especially handy for students who wish to record scores for you.

Correction Overhead:

Used to produce an overhead transparency for correcting assignments as a group. By projecting the numbered boxes onto the whiteboard, you'll have spaces for writing the answers without having to do it yourself. (See bottom of page 11.)

I Made a Good Choice:

These positive choice cards are xeroxed and then clipped together for easy handling. They are given out to students for meeting any of the goals stated on the form. Students may exchange one for a coupon if they bring it back with a parent signature. I offer two coupons if it also contains a comment from Mom or Dad. (See Wall of Fame, page 26.)

Student of the Day Award:

Reproduce on colorful paper and use for recognizing student behavior or achievement. It's best, when announcing the winner, to verbalize the behavior or achievement first. This way, the students will focus on the skill that's being acknowledged and not just the student who is receiving the award. (See Student of the Day, page 28.)

Student Bulletin:

Descriptions for use found on pages 32 and 62.

Counseling Center Log:

Description for use found on page 56.

Teacher/Student Agreement:

Description for use found on page 75.

Classroom Survival Rules:

Reproduce and post in your room. They probably won't follow all of the suggestions shown; nonetheless, it's fun to see it hanging on the wall.

	1	19
	2	20
	3	21
	4	22
	5	23
	6	24
	7	25
	8	26
	9	27
	10	28
	11	29
	12	30
	13	31
	14	32
	15	33
	16	34
	17	35
	18	36

	1	19
	2	20
	3	21
	4	22
	5	23
	6	24
	7	25
	8	26
	9	27
	10	28
	11	29
	12	30
	13	31
	14	32
	15	33
	16	34
	17	35
	18	36

	1	19
	2	20
	3	21
	4	22
	5	23
	6	24
	7	25
	8	26
	9	27
	10	28
	11	29
	12	30
	13	31
	14	32
	15	33
	16	34
	17	35
	18	36

	1	19
	2	20
	3	21
	4	22
	5	23
	6	24
	7	25
	8	26
	9	27
	10	28
	11	29
	12	30
	13	31
	14	32
	15	33
	16	34
	17	35
	18	36

ASSIGNMENT:

Mon	Tue	Wed	Thr	Fri	_____		at	_____
1	2	3	4	5	6	7	8	9	10	11	12
13	14	15	16	17	18	19	20	21	22	23	24
25	26	27	28	29	30	31	32	33	34	35	36

ASSIGNMENT:

Mon	Tue	Wed	Thr	Fri	_____		at	_____
1	2	3	4	5	6	7	8	9	10	11	12
13	14	15	16	17	18	19	20	21	22	23	24
25	26	27	28	29	30	31	32	33	34	35	36

ASSIGNMENT:

Mon	Tue	Wed	Thr	Fri	_____		at	_____
1	2	3	4	5	6	7	8	9	10	11	12
13	14	15	16	17	18	19	20	21	22	23	24
25	26	27	28	29	30	31	32	33	34	35	36

ASSIGNMENT:

Mon	Tue	Wed	Thr	Fri	_____		at	_____
1	2	3	4	5	6	7	8	9	10	11	12
13	14	15	16	17	18	19	20	21	22	23	24
25	26	27	28	29	30	31	32	33	34	35	36

ASSIGNMENT:

Mon	Tue	Wed	Thr	Fri	_____		at	_____
1	2	3	4	5	6	7	8	9	10	11	12
13	14	15	16	17	18	19	20	21	22	23	24
25	26	27	28	29	30	31	32	33	34	35	36

ACTIVITY

DATE	POSSIBLE SCORE		
1		19	
2		20	
3		21	
4		22	
5		23	
6		24	
7		25	
8		26	
9		27	
10		28	
11		29	
12		30	
13		31	
14		32	
15		33	
16		34	
17		35	
18		36	

ACTIVITY

DATE	POSSIBLE SCORE		
1		19	
2		20	
3		21	
4		22	
5		23	
6		24	
7		25	
8		26	
9		27	
10		28	
11		29	
12		30	
13		31	
14		32	
15		33	
16		34	
17		35	
18		36	

ACTIVITY

DATE	POSSIBLE SCORE		
1		19	
2		20	
3		21	
4		22	
5		23	
6		24	
7		25	
8		26	
9		27	
10		28	
11		29	
12		30	
13		31	
14		32	
15		33	
16		34	
17		35	
18		36	

CORRECTION OVERHEAD

01.	02.	03.	04.
05.	06.	07.	08.
09.	10.	11.	12.
13.	14.	15.	16.
17.	18.	19.	20.
21.	22.	23.	24.
25.	26.	27.	28.
29.	30.	31.	32.
33.	34.	35.	36.
37.	38.	39.	40.

I MADE A GOOD CHOICE

Name: _____

Date: _____ / _____ / _____

BEGINS WORK PROMPTLY	
COMPLETES WORK ON TIME	
WORKS COOPERATIVELY	
FOLLOWS DIRECTIONS	
LISTENS ATTENTIVELY	
DOES NEAT, CAREFUL WORK	
CLASSROOM BEHAVIOR	
PLAYGROUND BEHAVIOR	
RESPECTS RIGHTS OF OTHERS	
PRACTICES SELF-DISCIPLINE	

I made a really good choice today in class. Making good choices is making me a good student and a better person.

I MADE A GOOD CHOICE

Name: _____

Date: _____ / _____ / _____

BEGINS WORK PROMPTLY	
COMPLETES WORK ON TIME	
WORKS COOPERATIVELY	
FOLLOWS DIRECTIONS	
LISTENS ATTENTIVELY	
DOES NEAT, CAREFUL WORK	
CLASSROOM BEHAVIOR	
PLAYGROUND BEHAVIOR	
RESPECTS RIGHTS OF OTHERS	
PRACTICES SELF-DISCIPLINE	

I made a really good choice today in class. Making good choices is making me a good student and a better person.

I MADE A GOOD CHOICE

Name: _____

Date: _____ / _____ / _____

BEGINS WORK PROMPTLY	
COMPLETES WORK ON TIME	
WORKS COOPERATIVELY	
FOLLOWS DIRECTIONS	
LISTENS ATTENTIVELY	
DOES NEAT, CAREFUL WORK	
CLASSROOM BEHAVIOR	
PLAYGROUND BEHAVIOR	
RESPECTS RIGHTS OF OTHERS	
PRACTICES SELF-DISCIPLINE	

I made a really good choice today in class. Making good choices is making me a good student and a better person.

I MADE A GOOD CHOICE

Name: _____

Date: _____ / _____ / _____

BEGINS WORK PROMPTLY	
COMPLETES WORK ON TIME	
WORKS COOPERATIVELY	
FOLLOWS DIRECTIONS	
LISTENS ATTENTIVELY	
DOES NEAT, CAREFUL WORK	
CLASSROOM BEHAVIOR	
PLAYGROUND BEHAVIOR	
RESPECTS RIGHTS OF OTHERS	
PRACTICES SELF-DISCIPLINE	

I made a really good choice today in class. Making good choices is making me a good student and a better person.

I MADE A GOOD CHOICE

Name: _____

Date: _____ / _____ / _____

BEGINS WORK PROMPTLY	
COMPLETES WORK ON TIME	
WORKS COOPERATIVELY	
FOLLOWS DIRECTIONS	
LISTENS ATTENTIVELY	
DOES NEAT, CAREFUL WORK	
CLASSROOM BEHAVIOR	
PLAYGROUND BEHAVIOR	
RESPECTS RIGHTS OF OTHERS	
PRACTICES SELF-DISCIPLINE	

I made a really good choice today in class. Making good choices is making me a good student and a better person.

I MADE A GOOD CHOICE

Name: _____

Date: _____ / _____ / _____

BEGINS WORK PROMPTLY	
COMPLETES WORK ON TIME	
WORKS COOPERATIVELY	
FOLLOWS DIRECTIONS	
LISTENS ATTENTIVELY	
DOES NEAT, CAREFUL WORK	
CLASSROOM BEHAVIOR	
PLAYGROUND BEHAVIOR	
RESPECTS RIGHTS OF OTHERS	
PRACTICES SELF-DISCIPLINE	

I made a really good choice today in class. Making good choices is making me a good student and a better person.

I MADE A GOOD CHOICE

Name: _____

Date: _____ / _____ / _____

BEGINS WORK PROMPTLY	
COMPLETES WORK ON TIME	
WORKS COOPERATIVELY	
FOLLOWS DIRECTIONS	
LISTENS ATTENTIVELY	
DOES NEAT, CAREFUL WORK	
CLASSROOM BEHAVIOR	
PLAYGROUND BEHAVIOR	
RESPECTS RIGHTS OF OTHERS	
PRACTICES SELF-DISCIPLINE	

I made a really good choice today in class. Making good choices is making me a good student and a better person.

I MADE A GOOD CHOICE

Name: _____

Date: _____ / _____ / _____

BEGINS WORK PROMPTLY	
COMPLETES WORK ON TIME	
WORKS COOPERATIVELY	
FOLLOWS DIRECTIONS	
LISTENS ATTENTIVELY	
DOES NEAT, CAREFUL WORK	
CLASSROOM BEHAVIOR	
PLAYGROUND BEHAVIOR	
RESPECTS RIGHTS OF OTHERS	
PRACTICES SELF-DISCIPLINE	

I made a really good choice today in class. Making good choices is making me a good student and a better person.

STUDENT OF THE DAY

is awarded this certificate
for outstanding achievement.

R.A.D.

STUDENT OF THE DAY

is awarded this certificate
for outstanding achievement.

R.A.D.

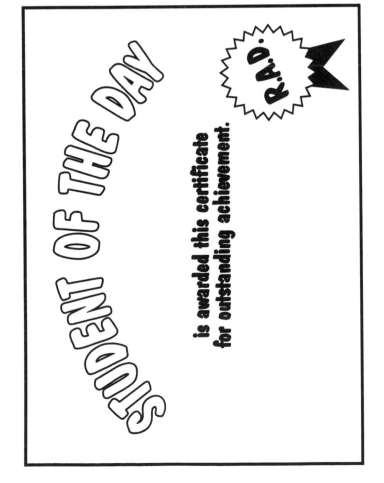

STUDENT OF THE DAY

is awarded this certificate
for outstanding achievement.

R.A.D.

STUDENT OF THE DAY

is awarded this certificate
for outstanding achievement.

R.A.D.

STUDENT BULLETIN

Name _____   Date _____

BEHAVIOR

- ❑ Demonstrated leadership
- ❑ Set good example
- ❑ Strived to improve
- ❑ Sometimes forgot self-control
- ❑ Placed on restriction
  for one day

- ❑ If checked here,
  please sign & return.

WORK HABITS

- ❑ Worked independently
- ❑ Showing improvement in
  work skills and study habits
- ❑ Needed some guidance to
  complete class assignments
- ❑ Needed constant guidance to
  complete class assignments
- ❑ Easily distracted
- ❑ Distracted others

EFFORT

- ❑ Excellent effort
- ❑ Very good effort
- ❑ Good effort
- ❑ Is improving
- ❑ Needs to improve

Conference requested
- ❑ by teacher
- ❑ by parent

Teacher signature _____   Parent signature _____

STUDENT BULLETIN

Name _____

Date _____

A **Red Hand** means:
- blurting out an answer
- not waiting to be called upon

A **Green Hand** means:
- raising a hand to speak
- waiting patiently for a turn

Teacher signature _____   Parent signature _____

Counseling Center

Name	Date	SB

Teacher/Student Agreement

Parent copy required: | YES | NO |

01	10	19	28
02	11	20	29
03	12	21	30
04	13	22	31
05	14	23	32
06	15	24	33
07	16	25	34
08	17	26	35
09	18	27	36

CLASSROOM SURVIVAL INSTRUCTIONS

If you open it,   close it.

If you turn it on,   turn it off.

If you break it,   fix it.

If you can't fix it,   get someone who can.

If you use it,   take care of it.

If it belongs to someone else,   get permission before you use it.

If you borrow it,   return it.

If you make a mess,   clean it up.

If you move it,   put it back.

If it doesn't concern you,   don't mess with it.

New Management Products

> "*Thanks for all of your life-saving tips. I haven't implemented them all yet, but so far, my students have responded to each and every one exactly like you said they would. The fun is back, and I am far less frazzled at the end of the day.*"

Sharon Snobeck   Oakley Elementary School   Santa Maria, California

In his newest book, Rick Morris shares the secrets to fifty of his exciting, innovative techniques dealing with Management, Motivation, Interaction, Student Numbers, and Team Based Teaching. *Tools & Toys* will add new life to your classroom, increase the level of student involvement, and reduce your stress on a daily basis.

100 pages, comes complete with a set of blackline masters $10.00

Order Form on Last Page

CLASS CARDS
A NEW MANAGEMENT TEACHING TOOL

3 Jason

Rick Morris

This delightful little book describes in detail the use of a teaching technique from the New Management system of classroom management and student motivation. The three chapters—Getting Started, Making It Work, and Card Tricks—offer clear and concise explanations for using this dynamic, interactive tool.

A refreshingly simple idea, CLASS CARDS will empower you to maximize the growth and development of each and every student. It will also enable you to maintain a teaching style which is fair, firm, and consistent: the hallmark of an effective educator.

70 pages, fully illustrated

$5.00

FLIP WRITER

The fun way to learn cursive! Just fan the pages of this book, and watch cursive letters come alive. Ideally suited for initial instruction, remediation, or as a handy reference guide for independent student use, this playful learning device will have your students forming letters properly in no time.

We guarantee that your class will love this book, or we'll buy it back!

$10.00

Book One: Lowercase Cursive

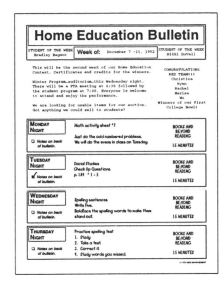

The Home Education Bulletin

The New Management System
for building a successful home learning program

This easy-to-follow teacher's guide will show you how to start your own homework communication tool for improving the quality and effort your students put into their home studies. A real parent favorite, The Home Education Bulletin comes complete with samples, suggestions, and a set of blackline masters.

$3.00

Teacher's Guide • Sample Bulletin

Grade Keeping Suggestions • Blackline Masters

Sentence Strips:
Cut and Paste Paragraphs

The New Management technique
for successful student writing

Sentence Strips is a new and powerful way for students to gain writing confidence and become more proficient writers. Originally published in *The Writing Notebook*, this revised version is a sixteen-page mini-guide which provides step-by-step instructions for incorporating this simple yet effective technique into your existing written language program.

$3.00

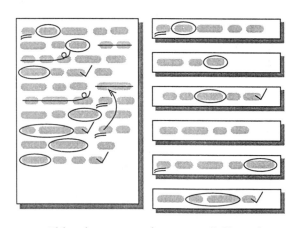

Old style paragraph writing (left) and
the Sentence Strip method (right).

DOOR BLØK

✓ WORKS WITH KNOBS OR HANDLES

✓ ELIMINATES BOTHERSOME DOOR NOISE

✓ REDUCES CLASSROOM DISTRACTIONS

✓ FACILITATES ENTRY FOR PHYSICALLY CHALLENGED STUDENTS

✓ HANGS FROM INTERIOR KNOB WHEN NOT IN USE

$5.00

Research Identifies Door as #1 Classroom Distraction

In a recent study on classroom distractions, the sound of the door opening and closing was found to be the biggest distraction of them all. That's why Rick Morris invented DOOR BLØK.

It's simple, functional design prevents the door from closing fully. Not only is the sound of the closing door gone, but so is the rattling of the knob as students come and go. A simple push or pull on the door and it opens and closes silently.

NEW MANAGEMENT ORDER FORM

For faster service,
please call Debra at 1-619-455-6000
or fax this form to 1-619-455-0011.

#	Product	Price	Cost
	Tools & Toys: Fifty Fun Ways to Love Your Class *Learn the secrets to 50 of Rick Morris's exciting, innovative classroom techniques. 100 pages, fully illustrated.*	10.00	
	Class Cards: A New Management Teaching Tool *This easy-to-use interactive teaching technique will add zip to your lessons and class discussions. 70 pages, fully illustrated.*	5.00	
	Flip Writer *The fun way to learn cursive! This playful book allows students to learn the art of cursive writing in a brand new way.*	10.00	
	The Home Education Bulletin *A sixteen-page teacher's guide for starting your own homework communication sheet. Blackline masters included.*	3.00	
	Sentence Strips *This step-by-step handbook will teach you a new and powerful way for your students to become more effective writers.*	3.00	
	DOOR BLØK *Heavy-duty rubber device which hooks over door knobs or handles and eliminates the sound of your classroom door.*	5.00	

Please note: Sales tax has already been included in the prices shown above.	SUB-TOTAL	
	SHIPPING & HANDLING	3.00
	TOTAL	

Make check payable to:

NEW MANAGEMENT

Mail check and order form to:

New Management
6512 Edmonton Avenue
San Diego, CA 92122

SHIP THIS ORDER TO:

Name

Address

City   State   ZIP